# BROOKLYN SPACES

## 50 HUBS OF CULTURE AND CREATIVITY

# BROOKLYN SPACES

## ORIANA LECKERT

Foreword by Jeff Stark

THE MONACELLI PRESS

Published in the United States by The Monacelli Press

Library of Congress Control Number
2014956678

ISBN 978-1-58093-428-2

Design by Suzanne LaGasa
Printed in China

10 9 8 7 6 5 4 3 2 1

www.monacellipress.com

# TABLE OF CONTENTS

# FOREWORD

## by Jeff Stark

*There's a door in the sidewalk. Or behind a roll-up gate. Or down some alley . . .*
*"Hurry," says a voice. "Get in here!" . . . And here you are.*

I don't care if it's three in the morning or three in the afternoon: I will never love a place more than the first time I see it. It's like stepping into another world—a secret revealed. Each new space makes my life bigger.

Oriana Leckert is the same way. You don't end up in many of the spaces in this book without looking for them. They're too far afield, in both geography and dream.

That means Oriana is an explorer. For years she and her photographers have gone to the outer edges of what were—for a time—the farther neighborhoods in Brooklyn and sent out reports. So there's a bit of frontier in this book, sort of like those great big paintings from the Old American West.

It's one of the reasons the people in this book look so good. Dancing in perfect light, or dripping with sweat: these are beautiful young people doing what beautiful young people have always done.

But those big paintings were romantic exaggerations. And you should also know that Brooklyn is not really like this book. Sorry. Our city is just like your city: there are chain stores and stadiums and horrible, horrible glass condos all over the place.

But we also have these precious fortresses in New York. These living experiments. These utopian glens, often hiding in trailer parks and dirty warehouses. Each with its own inhabitants. Each with its own customs. Holding on to what's left. Striking out for something new.

*Inside is another world . . . It's too hot. Or it's too cold. It kind of smells bad . . .*
*It is* nothing *like what you expected.*


I am not one of those people who thinks everything used to be better back when CBGB was around. Those are fighting words in New York, but it's true. To me, the best landmark in Brooklyn—hell, in New York—in the last 20 years is the new Silent Barn, and it's still a very new place.

So many of the places in this book are middle fingers to all those trolls who say that New York died back whenever. Give me a place based on big, messy, collective decisions, dreamt up and run by the people who want it most, over a filthy club for junkies falling over one other on the Bowery.

New York is not dead. There is still so much independent spirit. Look at these spaces. A warehouse full of clowns. A social club for people who like fishing and bluegrass. Two or three trapeze schools. The last American sideshow.

No matter how dirty, how ramshackle, these spaces are beautiful. And for every photo of a sequined dancer beaming in stage light, there's someone sweeping cigarette butts out of the gutter at 6 AM. What's special about the spaces in this book is that it's usually the same person.

You won't read a lot about curators and promoters here. Instead, you'll meet organizers, artists, and cofounders. And behind them are hundreds of hands that took care of a thousand chores. That's what do-it-yourself means: you know where the slop bucket is and what day the trash gets picked up.

Some of the places in this book are underground venues. That is not a posture. In New York, I don't use the word "underground" as a euphemism for "cool." I use it instead of "illegal." This is always a little hard to explain. But as you page through this book, you should know that sometimes you could go to jail for pouring a whiskey in New York. Or be fined over a dance floor. Or get shut down if your audience is too big. You probably think that's ridiculous, and I agree. But our mayors do not, nor do our cops.

I point this out as a reminder that at the very core of all these spaces there is a kind of bravery, a real risk, made by passionate people willing to put themselves on the line. Sometimes this is true in the fully legal places as well. Paying rent here is its own kind of impossible.

New York is still the center of the culture industry in the United States, but so many of these spaces are way more about culture than industry. And what's important about that is they're not stepping stones for artists to climb on their way up to Madison Square Garden.

They're much more like actual gardens, with artists planting and tending and reaping and sowing, year after year. It's no surprise that metaphor is taken so directly: you'll find gardens out back or on the roofs of several of these spaces; some of them actually *are* gardens. And all of them, in some way, nourish a community of artists and creative people. This is the hard-won lesson of each of these Brooklyn spaces: you get out of it what you put into it.


*Why are you even here? . . . Well, look at these people: they made it too . . .*
*And here you are . . . Together.*

. . .


Jeff Stark is the editor of Nonsense NYC, a weekly email list about independent arts and culture started in 2000. He also creates his own events in unusual spaces.

# INTRODUCTION

**The first time I went to what I would consider a Brooklyn space was in 1998,** as a wide-eyed New Jersey college sophomore. My fedora-wearing, clove-smoking, Harry Partch-listening roommate drove us into the bright shimmering chaos of Manhattan and then out again, over the Williamsburg Bridge and into dark, seemingly abandoned Brooklyn. Out of the car, we stumbled down a deserted Bedford Ave, through the shadowy, barbed-wire-edged night, over broken sidewalks and past abandoned lots, to the middle of a decrepit block: 70 North 6th Street, Galapagos Art Space. Just inside the door was a huge inky black pool; hung above it and reflected in its depths was a complicated silvery webbed sculpture. Sidling past the pool we edged into the space itself—a cacophony of light and revelry, concrete walled, dappled with sconced candles and fringed with velvet curtains. That night was pure revelation: it was the first time I experienced performance art, the first time I heard intentionally dissonant music, the first time I drank wine that wasn't Manischewitz at synagogue. It was a beautifully tumultuous introduction to underground culture, avant-garde creativity, and the power of a unique space to dramatically augment both.

Brooklyn is a massive place, both in terms of geographical reach and population density. With 2.5 million people in 71 square miles, if the borough were its own city, it would be the third or fourth largest in the United States—and it's also the fastest-growing in New York City. There is a deep, incredibly varied history of art and culture here, one that existed long before the world began taking notice of "Brooklyn cool" in the early 2000s. The aim of this book is not to document a century's worth of creative culture, but to trace a specific artistic renaissance that has manifested over the last twenty years. This movement tends to be localized in a handful of Brooklyn neighborhoods that were also important to the city's industrial history—Williamsburg, Bushwick, Dumbo, Gowanus, Red Hook. This book's focus on that small part of the borough is not intended to diminish the incredible artistic and cultural achievements throughout the rest of it, nor is my use of "Brooklyn" and "Brooklynites" meant to imply that this is one cohesive place populated by one specific kind of person. On the contrary, Brooklyn is vast and contains multitudes—far more than could fit in one or even a dozen books. This one aims only to document the Brooklyn I know, the Brooklyn that is mine, the Brooklyn that endlessly inspires me with its passion, innovation, and experimentation.

The scene chronicled herein began in early-1990s Williamsburg, a neighborhood that at the time was mostly desolate and scattered with dangerous and lawless zones. It was also beginning to see a slow influx of artists, as New York City's economy picked up and housing prices in Manhattan began to climb—enough to support a few galleries, the first being Minor Injury and Test Site, which opened in 1990 and 1991, respectively. On the more renegade side was the rise of the cultural movement Immersionism: seizing the opportunity offered by the neighborhood's many abandoned warehouses, hundreds of artists would come together to create multisensory, night-long "happenings," fashioning the spaces into gigantic interactive playgrounds full of installations, decorations, and performances. The most notorious of these were Cat's Head (1990), FlyTrap (1991), and Organism (1993). During the same period, the neighborhood's new creative community launched several more permanent spaces for parties and music and open mics, like El Sensorium, Lizard's Tail, Mighty Robot, Keep Refrigerated, Rubulad (p. 172), and the Old Dutch Mustard Factory, each of which offered its own unique mix of DIY resourcefulness, cultural appetite, and a wild artistic sensibility. These art spaces were different from traditional cultural venues in many ways: they were community gathering spaces first and enter-tainment venues second, they lacked corporate or financial backing, they paid little attention to municipal requirements, thus operating quasi-legally or altogether outside of the law. And they were cobbled together with little more than spit, glitter, and the combined stubbornness of the artists who kept them running until they got caught, ran out of money, or ran out of steam.

This concentration of creative experimentation wasn't just taking place in Williamsburg. In a story of massive transformation disproportionate to its size, Dumbo, a once-industrial neighborhood that had been almost entirely abandoned when manufacturing left in the 1980s, became home to a thriving artistic community in the late 1990s. This neighborhood's metamorphosis was much more intentionally orchestrated than Williamsburg's spontaneous bloom. Much of Dumbo's stratospheric rise can be credited to real estate mogul David Walentas, who runs Two Trees Management with his son Jed. Two Trees bought eleven inactive Dumbo factories—totaling more than 2 million square feet—in 1981, back when the entire neighborhood was still zoned for manufacturing use only. Then-Mayor Rudolph Giuliani rezoned the area residential in 1997, and the Walentases began their long game, enticing artists, performers, and other creative types to the burgeoning neighborhood, offering low or even no rent for a limited term to culture-makers like the experimental art gallery Smack Melon, the avant-garde theatre St. Ann's Warehouse, and the nonprofit d.u.m.b.o. arts center. Artists attract more artists; other early entrants on the Dumbo scene were DUMBA, a queer/anarchist music and performance space that opened in 1996, and GAle GAtes et al., a theatre group known for large-scale multimedia performances that opened in 1997. Also in 1997 was the first annual Art Under the Bridge festival, with open studio displays from about 100 artists; it is now known as Dumbo Arts Festival and was attended by more than 200,000 people in 2014.

By the 2000s, groundswells of cultural experimentation were coursing through many other neighborhoods across Brooklyn. The borough began transforming from a place for creative people to mark time on the way to Manhattan into the destination itself, the very height of creative aspiration, with wave after wave of DIY music venues, unusual performance spaces, experiments in radical communal living, and whimsical repurposing of industrial buildings. As the open-source movement careened out of the tech industry and into other facets of cultural life, artists and artisans began creating innovative skillshares, working together to teach and learn everything from robotics to tintype photography. By the end of the aughts, Brooklyn was internationally known for its raucous, illicit warehouse parties, unique hipster stylings, innovative foodies, and cutting-edge music. From performance to fashion, from literature to booze, the borough had become an unstoppable force for both the incubation and arbitration of taste across the cultural spectrum.

The spaces in this book demonstrate a cross-section of life in Brooklyn (and just a little bit beyond), from quirky museums to experimental art collectives to maker labs. These are not just physical locations with creative people in them; a Brooklyn Space embodies an ethos that combines creativity, culture, and community. Each is an unexpected space repurposed into a hub where like-minded people gather to support and inspire one another. For trapezists there's a state-of-the-art aerial skillshare in a former ice warehouse (p. 104), for classical musicians, a venue in a former firehouse (p. 66), for amateur biologists, a lab in a corner of a massive former bank (p. 90). In this book you'll also find fascinations like an art collective in a 19th-century schoolhouse (p. 178), a metalworking shop in a repurposed cannonball factory (p. 94), a yoga collective in a onetime chicken slaughterhouse (p. 24), and an experimental distillery in one of the oldest manufacturing complexes in the country (p. 110). In addition to illuminating the people who run and use these spaces, I've done my best to trace each one's history, from its industrial or commercial past to its artistic present. Many of these spaces have taken on a palimpsestic quality, as one group of artists after another attempts to make something beautiful that they can hold on to against New York's catastrophically rising rents and increasingly draconian enforcement by city authorities.

Because the sad truth is that Brooklyn has in many ways become a victim of its own success. Betting correctly on the moneymaking potential of the borough, in 2006 then-Mayor Michael Bloomberg rezoned wide swaths of the North Brooklyn waterfront, ushering in an unprecedented real estate development spree that saw average housing prices in Williamsburg increase more than 175 percent from 2004 to 2012—pushing out longtime neighborhood residents, then the artists who replaced them, then even the middle-income earners who replaced *them*. Dumbo, once a post-industrial outpost sparsely populated by a few creative groups, has been entirely transformed into a bustling hive of chic shops, innovative tech startups, and luxury loft conversions, where space is now valued up to $1,000 per square foot—quite a jump from the $6 per square foot David Walentas paid in 1981.

This book was written over the summer of 2014, a time that felt like the culmination of a crisis, a tipping-point moment when Brooklyn was shifting irrevocably from a place of rampant innovation and thriving culture to one of hyper-gentrification paired with a total disinterest in preserving underground nightlife and artistic experimentation. New York City has long been marked by the tension between the high cost of living and the masses of creative people trying to succeed here while pursuing nontraditional lifestyles, but vast swaths of Brooklyn are now completely out of reach for all but the most well-heeled. The expense and complexity of doing business have also increased dramatically, with neighborhoods that were filled with art spaces and experimental playhouses a decade ago now cluttered with bank branches, high-end clothing boutiques, and international chains—the kind of businesses that can afford the five-figure monthly rents. The last five years have seen the shuttering of a nearly endless parade of DIY music venues, including long-running notables like 285 Kent, Glasslands, Monster Island, Market Hotel, Dead Herring, Port D'Or, and Newsonic. Legendary underground spaces for art parties and spectacles like the Old Dutch Mustard Factory, Rubulad, Red

Lotus Room, 12-Turn-13, and Broken Angel have been priced out or pushed out, many torn down to make way for luxury condos. We've lost community gardens, renegade boats, living room galleries, socialist cafés, queer collective houses, avant-garde puppet theatres, and on and on and on. By the time this book is published we will have lost more—including, certainly, some within these pages.

Of course, underground and DIY spaces are by their nature tenuous and fleeting. And or all those that have acquiesced to building code violations, lack of adequate licensing, and an inability or unwillingness to work within New York City's financial requirements, there are also many that are still here, with thriving communities continuing to innovate and create within their walls. It's all the more incredible to witness the tenacity of spaces that are still fighting, some in their second or even third incarnations. Spaces like Silent Barn (p. 186), House of Yes (p. 104), Galapagos Art Space (p. 82), and Cloud City (p. 54) have found ways to evolve rather than die, to achieve legitimacy and staying power despite a deck that seems increasingly stacked against them.

I've spent the last decade in Brooklyn, and have been chronicling this facet of its creative renaissance since 2010 on my website, brooklyn-spaces.com. I've had the incredible opportunity to visit count-less inspiring spaces and speak to the scores of outrageously passionate people driving them. I hope that each page of this book imparts the thrilled sense of wonder I've felt walking into every single one of these spaces, for the first time or the fiftieth, as well as an absolute amazement that they have man-aged to exist at all, that one person or several created these extraordinary things out of thin air, using their own particular mixture of vision, stubbornness, and drive. I've tried to capture the essence of a phenomenon, a cultural history of a creative renaissance in the midst of its kaleidoscopic, frenetic glory, before all of it, perhaps, is gone.

# BATCAVE

**One of the last truly wild places in an** increasingly sanitized Brooklyn, the Batcave was one of the longest-running squats in the borough. Colonized by around fifty people in its mid-2000s heyday, the enormous derelict space became an internationally known destination for urban exploration, a mecca for graffiti artists, and a source of fascination for anyone interested in renegade living situations.

A proud relic of Gowanus' industrial past, the space itself is an absolute behemoth: 24,000 square feet, three stories, forty-foot ceilings, and a thirteen-foot concrete slab floor that extends below the water table. Built in the late 1880s on the bank of the Gowanus Canal—some say on top of a Revolutionary War–era graveyard—the building was originally occupied by Nassau Sulfur Works, according to early city maps. Ownership was transferred to Brooklyn Rapid Transit in 1904 for use as a coal-fired power station for the trolleys, then to the Williamsburg Power Plant Corporation in 1938 for use as a central power station, and finally to the MTA in 1950, which used it as an electrical sub-station and switching yard until 1996.

By the early 2000s, the building had been abandoned for a half-dozen years. Zac E., a teenage runaway who later became an EMT, was brought there in 2001 by a friend—"It was wide open, we just walked right in"—and he and a few others began sleeping there regularly. "We set up a couple of rooms, dragging in mattresses and other furniture in the middle of the night," Zac says. Word of the nascent squat began to spread, and by 2002 there were about twenty punks, artists, musicians, and travelers living in dozens of little rooms crafted out of pallets, tarps, and industrial detritus. Zac brought in his photographer girlfriend Tanya P., and though she was at first terrified by the building's seeming menace, she quickly fell in love with its rawness and decrepit beauty.

A tight camaraderie developed, focusing on mutual aid and respect. The residents carved out kitchens, living rooms, and a bike-building shop; they pirated electricity from the Carroll Street Bridge, built rainwater bucket-flush toilets with help from veteran Lower East Side squatters, and fashioned a kerosene stove that ran off of paint thinner. "The community was really strong," Zac says. "We'd dumpster-dive for food and cook dinner together. We'd make art together, like a life-size chess board and huge hanging mobiles." They also threw parties and shows, with bands like Unstoppable Death Machines, CrackBox, Violent Sects, and Napalm Donut. The building continued to be a graffiti destination, with lurid murals and wild-style tags covering all available space, as well as radical slogans—END STOP AND FRISK, FUCK WALL STREET, OPEN YOUR EYES—painted huge on the exterior façade, visible from the passing elevated F and G trains.

The earnest young squatters eked out a peaceful existence for several years. "It was kind of like a pirate ship that wasn't on the water, a place where anyone was welcome if you could find a way in, where you could create a little world to live in," says Tanya. But in 2004, there was a crackdown on squats across the city; Kung Fu Castle on the Bowery was torn down to make way for luxury condos, and Casa del Sol, established in 1984 in the South Bronx, burned to the ground mere hours after a sudden eviction by the city. With fewer places left to go, squatters began flocking to the Batcave in greater numbers, and it became difficult for the original group to maintain the happy, collaborative atmosphere they'd created. "It worked until the people who didn't give a shit outnumbered the people who did," Zac says. "After a certain point, it just wasn't worth it anymore." He and Tanya moved out in 2005.

In 2006 the *Daily News* ran a sensationalist story breathlessly decrying the Batcave as a haven for violent junkies. The owner of the building had been working on plans to develop a luxury housing complex there called Gowanus Village, and within days of the article, the doors were welded shut and security guards were patrolling the grounds. But Gowanus Village was not to be, and by 2008, Batcave was on the market for $27 million. It didn't sell until 2012—for a mere $7 million—and, in a shocking twist for today's Brooklyn real estate narrative, the man who bought it, famously reclusive philanthropist Joshua Reichnitz, seems to have no intention of turning it into condos, luxury or otherwise.

Reichnitz steadfastly refuses interviews and shuns publicity, but he has made it known that his intentions for the Batcave are to remake it into something befitting its creative legacy: a community gathering and exhibition space with room inside for more than fifty art studios. According to a *New York Times* article published shortly after the sale, Reichnitz and his partner in the project, Randy Polumbo, "plan to keep the essential rawness of the Batcave," after fixing its crumbling interior and making it safe to be inside. It remains to be seen whether this will be possible, and what will become of the derelict colossus. "I feel like the building itself will have the final say," Tanya says. "People are trying to tame it, but it seems like it doesn't really want to be touched or domesticated. It's too wild."

Although the Batcave was unequivocally illegal, the squatter community that called it home for so many years exemplified the strong imperative to construct a home and family by any means necessary, a feeling often prevalent in alienating and lonely urban environments. It's creative place-making at its finest: an anarchic coming together of passionate, like-minded people, intensely motivated to help one another pull together the trappings of an exuberant, fulfilling life in the unlikeliest of places.

*Photos by Jon and Tanya*

CLOCKWISE FROM TOP LEFT: A group of squatters gather around a contained fire; Zac E. returns to the Batcave years after the squatter community vacated the space; remains of one of the many art projects that lingered long after the building's denizens departed.

For decades the Batcave was an internationally renowned destination for graffiti artists. The crumbling edifice teemed, inside and out, with murals, tags, and art pieces, ranging from the lurid to the political.

# BIG IRV'S

NEIGHBORHOOD
South Williamsburg

YEAR OPENED
2012

TYPE OF SPACE
Art collective

ORIGINAL USE
Bodega

WEBSITE
bigirvsgallery.com

**In 2010 twenty-five artists attempted** an unusual living experiment: they installed a dozen salvaged trailers into a former nut-roasting factory in the East Williamsburg Industrial Park, repurposing each into a bedroom or studio. Throughout the huge warehouse they also fashioned a darkroom, a woodworking shop, a koi pond, and a huge central gallery for art exhibitions and performances. Of course, New York City is not generally fond of radical living experiments, and the Bushwick Project for the Arts had a very short life; the Department of Buildings evicted the group a little more than a year after the experiment began.

After the trailer park's demise, half the group moved into a repurposed office building in Greenpoint, but it was sold two years later and the artists scattered again. Several settled in a South Williamsburg storefront, which over the years had been a bodega, a supermarket, a hardware store, and a small Pentecostal church.

In 2012 it became Big Irv's art collective. "I can't live in any other situation anymore," says musician and designer Damon Pelletier, who has been part of all these spaces. "I like being part of a community, in a space where everyone is helping each other out."

Nine artists, writers, and musicians live at Big Irv's, along with a dog and two pet rats. There's a shared studio in the basement, and the storefront/living room doubles as an art gallery and performance space. "People often wander in and ask if we're selling antiques, or if this is a reality show," says painter Kaitlyn Stubbs. But the collective members enjoy being visible, because it helps them meet and connect with their neighbors. "I'm sure they find us amusing," says Damon. "But whenever we barbecue, they'll throw some pork chops on the grill and join us."

The collective members have a wide range of talents and practices, from painting to ethnomusicology to fashion design, and these differing

Big Irv's monthly showcase features a variety of cultural entertainment, including curated visual art shows, poetry and prose readings, and music performances.

TOP: When Bushwick's Bodega Bar closed, its popular Live Storytelling Extravaganza was relocated to Big Irv's. INSET: All the Big Irv's denizens. BOTTOM: The storefront space inhabited by the collective.

The tiles in the building's entranceway spell out I. SHAPIRO & CO., which is where the name Big Irv's came from. The roommates have tried to investigate who I. Shapiro was, but so far have not found anything conclusive.

artistic sensibilities lead to a variety of events. There are visual art exhibitions, film screenings, a reading series brought over from the Bodega Bar in Bushwick, and a monthly music and art showcase. "Each of us brings something to the table, and curation of the space is a very collaborative effort," says writer Adam Selbst. The group also accepts proposals from emerging artists for installations and solo shows.

Part of the attraction of communal living is knowing there's always something interesting happening at home, from karaoke Thanksgivings to a tradition of Trailer Park Cake, a ladyfingers-and-fruit confection that can't be sliced and put on plates: "Everyone just grabs a fork and goes for it together," says Damon. And when one Big Irv's collective member put on a fashion show in Amsterdam, the rest of the group woke up at 6am to watch the livestream together and support her in real time.

"New York can be very isolating, and when you're isolated, you can start to feel a bit listless," says editor Mark DeLucas. "Living with a lot of people like this is really energizing." Kaitlyn feels similarly; after spending a year in an artist residency in Germany, she was nervous about returning to New York without a built-in social network. "For me, community is huge," she says. "And being able to have that community in my own home, as well as a studio and space to do events—it's a dream come true."

*Photos by Shannon*

# BIG SKY WORKS

**NEIGHBORHOOD**
Williamsburg

**YEAR OPENED**
2010

**TYPE OF SPACE**
Performance venue

**ORIGINAL USE**
Mechanic shop

**WEBSITE**
bigskyworksbrooklyn.com

**It seems like it's not a true Brooklyn** warehouse party unless there's an aerialist or two twirling about overhead. North Brooklyn is rife with acrobatic training spaces, from the Streb Lab for Action Mechanics to the House of Yes (p. 104) to The Muse (p. 142). But when veteran circus performer Tanya Gagné opened the Trapeze Loft in Williamsburg in 1999—in a space that had been Annie Heron's Test Site, one of the neighborhood's first commercial art galleries, from 1991 to 1993—she was pretty much the only game in town.

Tanya has been a professional circus performer for most of her life, gracing stages from Bard College's Spiegeltent to the Sydney Opera House in award-winning shows like La Soirée and La Clique. She's also one half of the internationally acclaimed bawdy burlesque/acrobatic duo the Wau Wau Sisters. She arrived in Williamsburg in 1992, when it was still mostly derelict: "This place was full of crack and hookers and cars on fire," she says. "Rent was $300 a month, and if you wanted to put on a show, you just went into a abandoned building and put on a show." Tanya lived in the art space Keep Refrigerated, near the Old Dutch Mustard Factory; both of these semi-abandoned warehouses were staging sites for all manner of illicit and strange art events, performances, and parties, and both were demolished in the mid-2000s to make room for condos.

When Tanya started the Trapeze Loft, she thought she might offer a handful of private lessons to a few curious Brooklynites, but the early 2000s saw the start of a huge interest in circus performance as a nightlife novelty, with high-profile bars, clubs, and music venues clamoring for acrobatic acts. Demand for Tanya's training turned out to be huge. The class offerings grew with the increased interest—acrobatics, hula-hoop, contortion, wire-walking, aerial silks, trapeze—and the tiny space couldn't expand to keep up. So in 2010 Tanya moved operations into a raw former mechanics shop on the northern edge of Williamsburg. In addition to an ever-widening roster of classes, she wanted Big Sky Works to serve as a venue for alternative music and unusual performance events, since the Williamsburg waterfront rezoning had shuttered so many others. "Gentrification doesn't have to mean this neighborhood can't be kooky anymore," she says.

The underground arts community rallied to help Tanya bring Big Sky Works to life. "One of my students who's a welder said, 'I'll weld the balcony railing!' Then one of my friends who's a carpenter said, 'I'll build the stage!'" More friends helped install lights, sound, and rigging. "It was like a tiny village all coming together," Tanya says. "People love this space because they can feel the energy that went into its creation, and that it was built for them to enjoy."

Big Sky Works now presents a grand variety of shows, with acrobatics, freakshow stunts, live visuals, disturbing clowns, contortionists, burlesque, drag, and an array of alternative music (Sean Lennon, Morgan O'Kane, and Kyp Malone have all performed). "This isn't just a circus space," says Tanya. "It's a funhouse, a theatre, a blank canvas. Whatever you want to try out, bring it here, we'll see how we can make it happen. I want to make sure we keep some artistic freedom, celebration, and curiosity in Williamsburg."

*Photos by Maximus and Ventiko*

Scenes from "Return of the Cunning Stunts," 2014. CLOCKWISE FROM TOP LEFT: Marawa Wamp; founder Tanya Gagné and Mark Winmill; Fez Faanana; circus accouterments awaiting use.

FROM TOP: Tanya as one half of the Wau Wau Sisters; Mark Winmill; a student showcase performance.

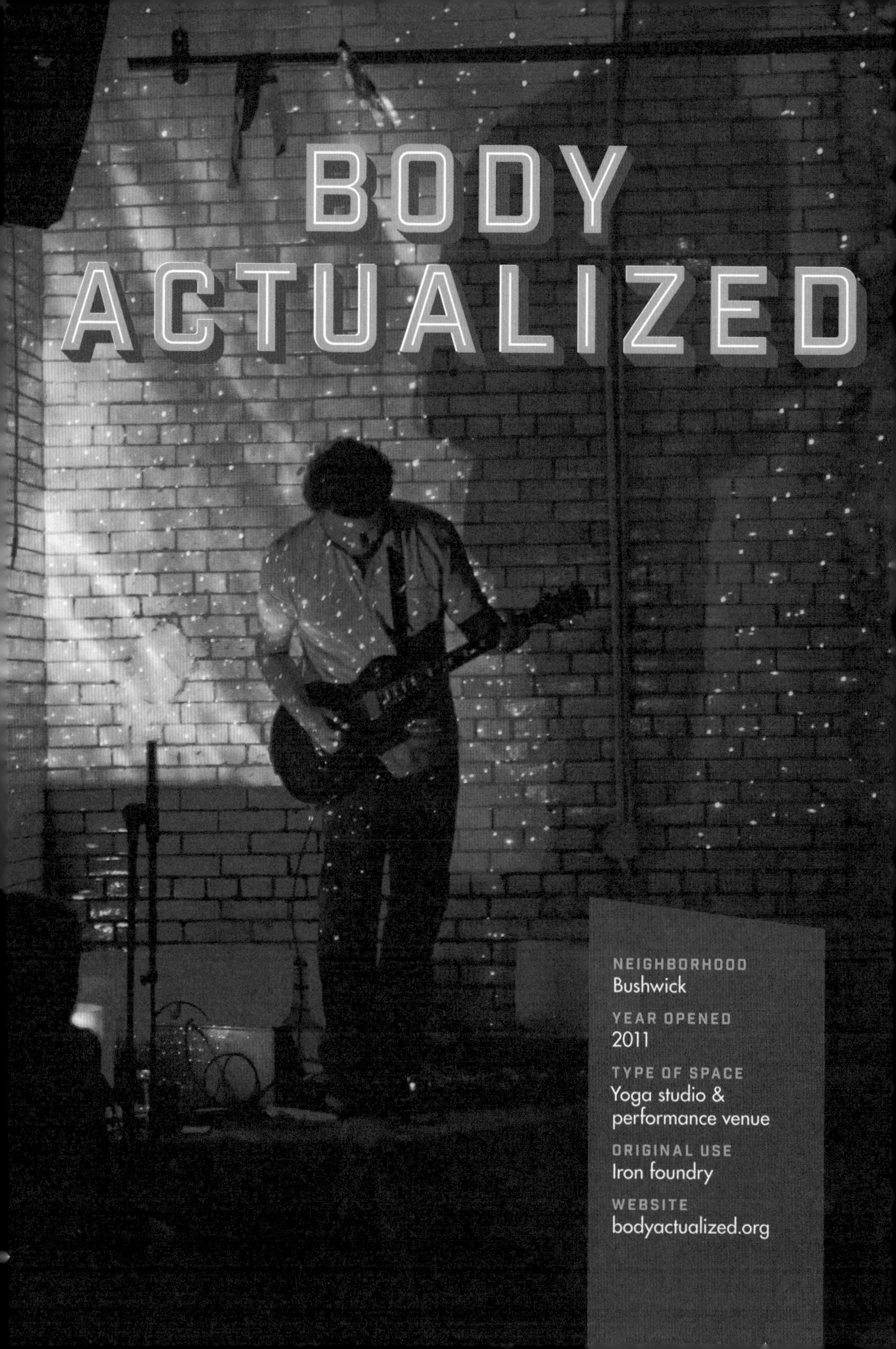

# BODY ACTUALIZED

**NEIGHBORHOOD**
Bushwick

**YEAR OPENED**
2011

**TYPE OF SPACE**
Yoga studio &
performance venue

**ORIGINAL USE**
Iron foundry

**WEBSITE**
bodyactualized.org

**"This space is kind of an oasis, one that's** so needed in this often isolating city," says Brian Sweeny, one of Body Actualized's founding members. A former iron foundry (then, briefly, a chicken slaughterhouse), the center is now a yoga studio and event space with reclaimed-wood floors and a wall of windows, filled with candles, incense, and piles of thick cushions. Run by a loose collective of musicians, artists, and promoters—several of whom make up Vibes Management, an event planning and promotion group whose focus is electronic music shows—the collective is non-hierarchical and dedicated to "radical honesty." All decisions about the space are made by consensus. "The rule is that no one should do anything they don't want to," says Brian. "That way everyone can be happy."

Several of the collective members teach yoga, and "everyone is into yoga as a way of life," says Brian. That's not a strict requirement, however: "Yoga is a small facet of a larger vibe and intention, just one core element in galvanizing the overall energy of what we're doing." During the day the space is used for hatha, vinyasa, and prana yoga, as well as rejuvenation and qi-yo workshops, new moon and full moon ceremonies, tarot readings, and shamanic astrology. "The classes are eclectic, but we all know what's appropriate for the space and what falls under the purview of our vibe," Brian says.

The group is also known for Cosmic Yoga, accompanied by live ambient electronic music, which existed well before the space opened in 2011. Under the name Body Actualized Control, the collective led Cosmic Yoga on the rooftop of the Market Hotel, an early Bushwick DIY music venue that was shut down by the city in 2010.

By night, the space becomes a venue for electronic music performances, poetry readings, and chill-out parties. Rather than booze, libations on offer include kombucha, organic juices, and

ABOVE: The Body Actualized altar is the group's way of honoring everyone who enters the space. It includes a central image of the cosmos because the space is "dedicated to all and the whole gorgeous chaotic shebang," says cofounder Anna Fitzgerald. It is continually reconfigured by different aesthetic impulses, "which is pretty divinely democratic."

Scenes from the Triptych performance series. ABOVE: Jocelyn Spaar reads poetry. BELOW: Todd Anderson composes both live and prerecorded multimedia sound and code projections.

a variety of teas. "It's positive nightlife with a cosmic aesthetic," says Brian. "Everything is working on a subtle level to open the pathways for someone's mind to travel to a different region." The collective's focus on "healthy hedonism," community empowerment, consciousness raising, creative opportunities, and spiritual growth draws a diverse array of people to the space. "It attracts people who think about the world in ways that weren't taught in high school," Brian says. "By doing unique things, we open people up to new possibilities."

*Photos by Kit and Maximus*

ABOVE: The team leaves valuable or meaningful objects out during performances in a gesture of trust and nonattachment. BELOW: By night Body Actualized is a venue for "positive nightlife," with DJs and musicians playing cosmic and electronic music to a relaxed audience.

# BROOKLYN BRAINERY

**NEIGHBORHOOD**
Carroll Gardens,
Prospect Heights

**YEAR OPENED**
2010, 2013

**TYPE OF SPACE**
Skillshare

**ORIGINAL USE**
Gym, ice cream parlor

**WEBSITE**
brooklynbrainery.com

In Brooklyn you can find an expert on absolutely anything, and chances are good that that person would love to share her expertise with others. Chances are also excellent that there are at least a dozen Brooklynites who would love to spend a couple of hours learning about that thing. That's the premise behind the Brooklyn Brainery, which offers inexpensive classes on a wildly eclectic range of things, from the history of anthropomorphic taxidermy to the science of cheese, from Shibori tie-dying to making *kokedama*, living moss balls.

Founders Jen Messier and Jonathan Soma had the idea for the Brainery in 2009. They both loved learning and attended classes whenever they could, but the offerings were expensive and often geared toward certification or licensing for professionals. "We wanted to learn about things like welding or shoemaking," Soma says, "but we were never planning to become welders or cobblers. We just wanted to know a little bit more." So the pair decided to give hobbyists and dabblers of all stripes an opportunity to pay a little to learn a little. "To be honest, we started it mostly to give ourselves an excuse to learn more," Jen says.

The Brainery opened in 2010 and was nomadic for a year, under rented space for classes by the hour at various studios and coworking spaces. But Jen and Soma knew they wouldn't be able to grow without their own home, so they raised $10,000 on Kickstarter and began looking for a base. It took quite a while; as Soma says, "in New York, finding a good space is probably harder than finding ten grand." Eventually they found a storefront at the southeastern corner of Carroll Gardens where they stayed for two years, building their reputation as Brooklyn's home for quirky education on any topic under the sun. In the beginning it was a challenge to find teachers, since it wasn't always easy to convince people that others would be interested in whatever obscure topic they were passionate about, so Soma taught about half the classes himself. "It's always been an eccentric mix of stuff," he says. "I taught Thai food and Norse mythology and the science of perception. I teach so much that I forget everything."

In 2013 the Brainery moved to its new home in Prospect Heights, in a storefront that had been an ice cream parlor in the 1950s, a deli in the '80s, and Impact Theatre in the '90s. Soma and Jen are thrilled with their new neighborhood. "It's just a very friendly, open place," says Jen. With a more malleable space, a big backyard, and the idea of open-source education firmly cemented in the Brooklyn consciousness, the Brainery's offerings have continued to increase and vary, from urban forestry to microwave candy to Haitian Creole. "The DIY education movement has convinced people that yes, they have knowledge worth sharing, and yes, they're capable of sharing it with other people," Soma says.

The combination of quirk, collaboration, and DIY resourcefulness is the kind of amalgam that Brooklyn is well known for, which isn't lost on the Brainery-ers. "We're totally a product of our environment," Jen says. "I don't think we'd be doing this if we lived somewhere else." Soma agrees: "I think it's just hilariously Brooklyn what we do. But we're totally self-aware and we love it."

*Photos by Jen*

An array of the many unusual classes offered at the Brainery. THIS PAGE, CLOCKWISE FROM TOP: Paper Architecture; Paper Marbling; Board Game Olympics. OPPOSITE: Design Thinking; Science of Perception.

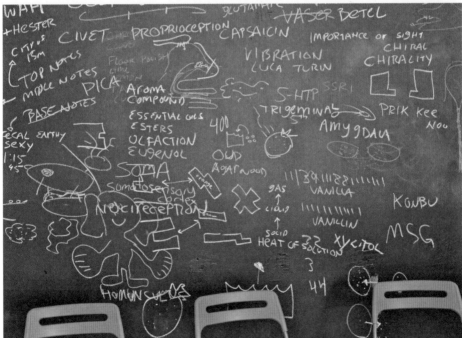

# BROOKLYN KITCHEN

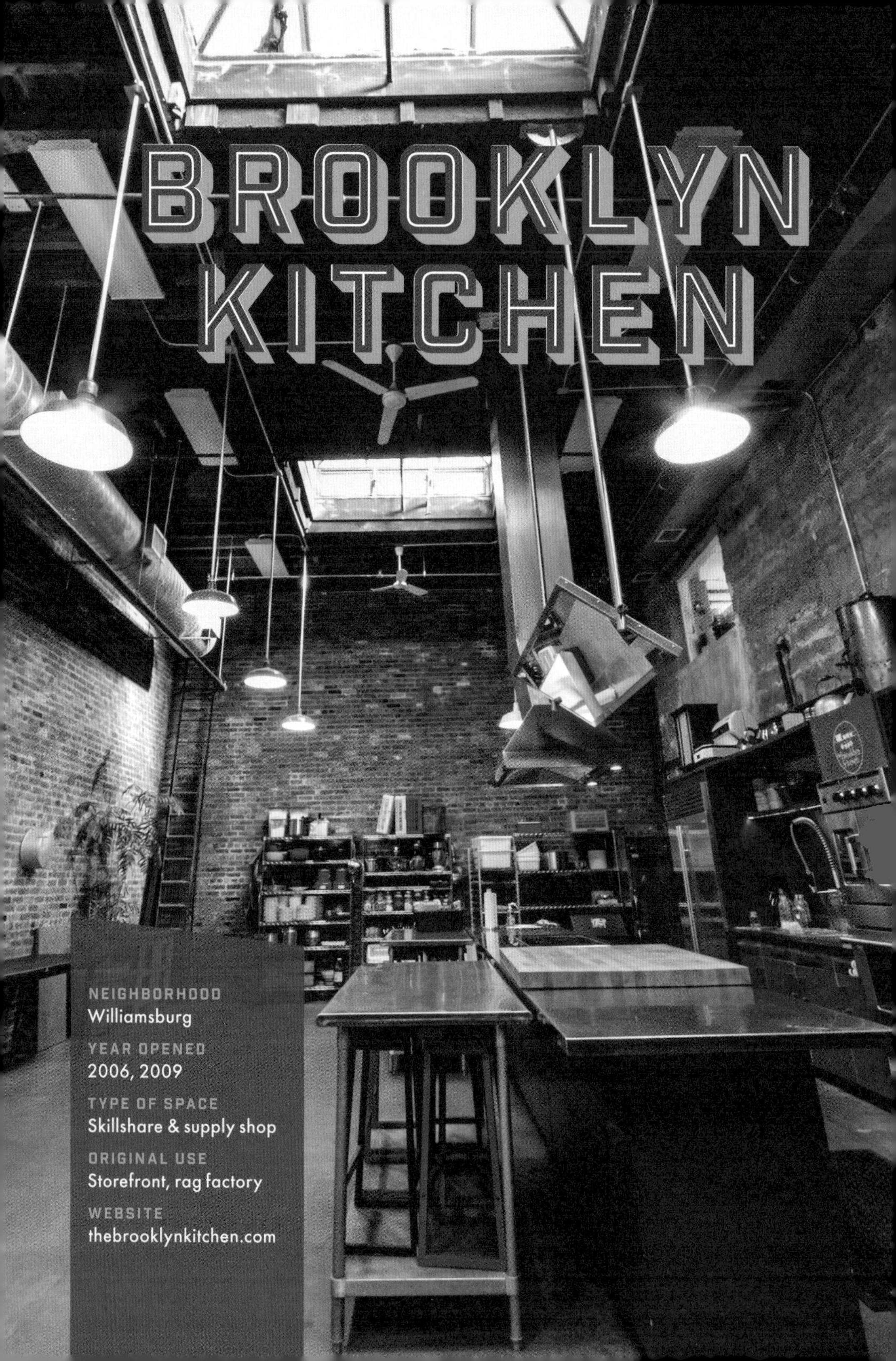

**NEIGHBORHOOD**
Williamsburg

**YEAR OPENED**
2006, 2009

**TYPE OF SPACE**
Skillshare & supply shop

**ORIGINAL USE**
Storefront, rag factory

**WEBSITE**
thebrooklynkitchen.com

**"We're so excited to get people cooking!"**
says Taylor Erkkinen, who cofounded Brooklyn Kitchen with her husband Harry Rosenblum. That enthusiasm is apparent in every corner of this carefully curated paean to all things food and drink. Densely packed with unusual goods and accessories, the shop represents a very Brooklyn approach to foodie culture: with a strong focus on teaching and skillsharing, its goal is to help turn any novice into a gourmand.

Taylor and Harry started the shop in 2006 in a tiny storefront. "We wanted it to be a seamless, thorough experience," says Taylor. "People should be able to choose a steak, buy a cast-iron pan, and sign up for a knife skills class all at the same time." But the space was so small that they could only stock a fraction of what they wanted to sell, and they had to close the shop

altogether to hold classes for a dozen people, at most. So three years in, the couple started looking for someplace new. As soon as they walked into a former rag factory under the BQE, they knew that they'd found their new home. Taylor was nine-months pregnant when they signed the lease, but they still managed to build everything out and open for business just four months later.

Embracing their completist desires, Taylor and Harry have stocked their shelves with everything imaginable for cooking, baking, brewing, pickling, seasoning, canning, slicing, or dicing. There are more than twenty-five kinds of bitters and a wall of knives that are unavailable anywhere else outside of Japan (Harry is "crazy obsessed" with knives, says Taylor). There's salt in a half-dozen exotic types (black Cyprus, blush Alaea) and KitchenAid mixers in every

OPPOSITE: One of Brooklyn Kitchen's two teaching kitchens. ABOVE: The Meat Hook, a butcher shop that stocks locally sourced meats from small family-owned farmers, is the Brooklyn Kitchen's "sister business": it was started out of the original Kitchen and continues to operate inside the shop.

color. There are starter kits for everything from dandelion wine to kimchi to kombucha. They sell vinegar by the barrel, dish soap in bulk, Yuzu marmalade from Japan, and a range of cheeses from San Francisco's Cowgirl Creamery. And naturally there are products from dozens of Brooklyn makers, like Brooklyn Slate Co., Salty Road , Mike's Hot Honey, Liddabit Sweets, Empire Mayo, and many more. Famed Brooklyn butchery the Meat Hook shares the space, selling beef, lamb, pork, six types of bacon, and fifty kinds of sausage.

And that's just the retail side. The two big teaching kitchens are the heart of the space, giving Brooklyn food aficionados a forum to share and improve their skills. Some popular classes include pickling with McClure's, pizza with Roberta's, cocktails with Tom Macy of the Clover Club, and whole-pig butchering with The Meat Hook, all highly regarded local outfits;

there are also classes on basics like bread making and menu planning, ethnic offerings from Bavaria to Vietnam, couples classes, and themed cooking competitions, like the Cupcake Bake-Off, the Meatball Smackdown, and the Bodega Challenge, where contestants make a meal for $10 using only ingredients available at the corner store.

"We try to serve people who are curious, who are figuring it out for themselves," Taylor says. "We're equipped to help you make whatever you want, as long as you're passionate about doing it." Their enthusiasm is contagious. "The best part of this job," Taylor says, "is when people come back to the store and say, 'You were right, this pan *did* change my life!'"

*Photos by Maximus*

CLOCKWISE FROM TOP: "Date Night: Taste of Spain" cooking class; coat hooks made of repurposed kitchen accessories; some of Brooklyn Kitchen's huge selection of imported knives.

CLOCKWISE FROM TOP: The shop's vast array of cooking items; the functional 2,000-pound scale left over from the building's past life as a rag factory; oils and vinegars sold in bulk.

# BROOKLYN
# ROD & GUN
# CLUB

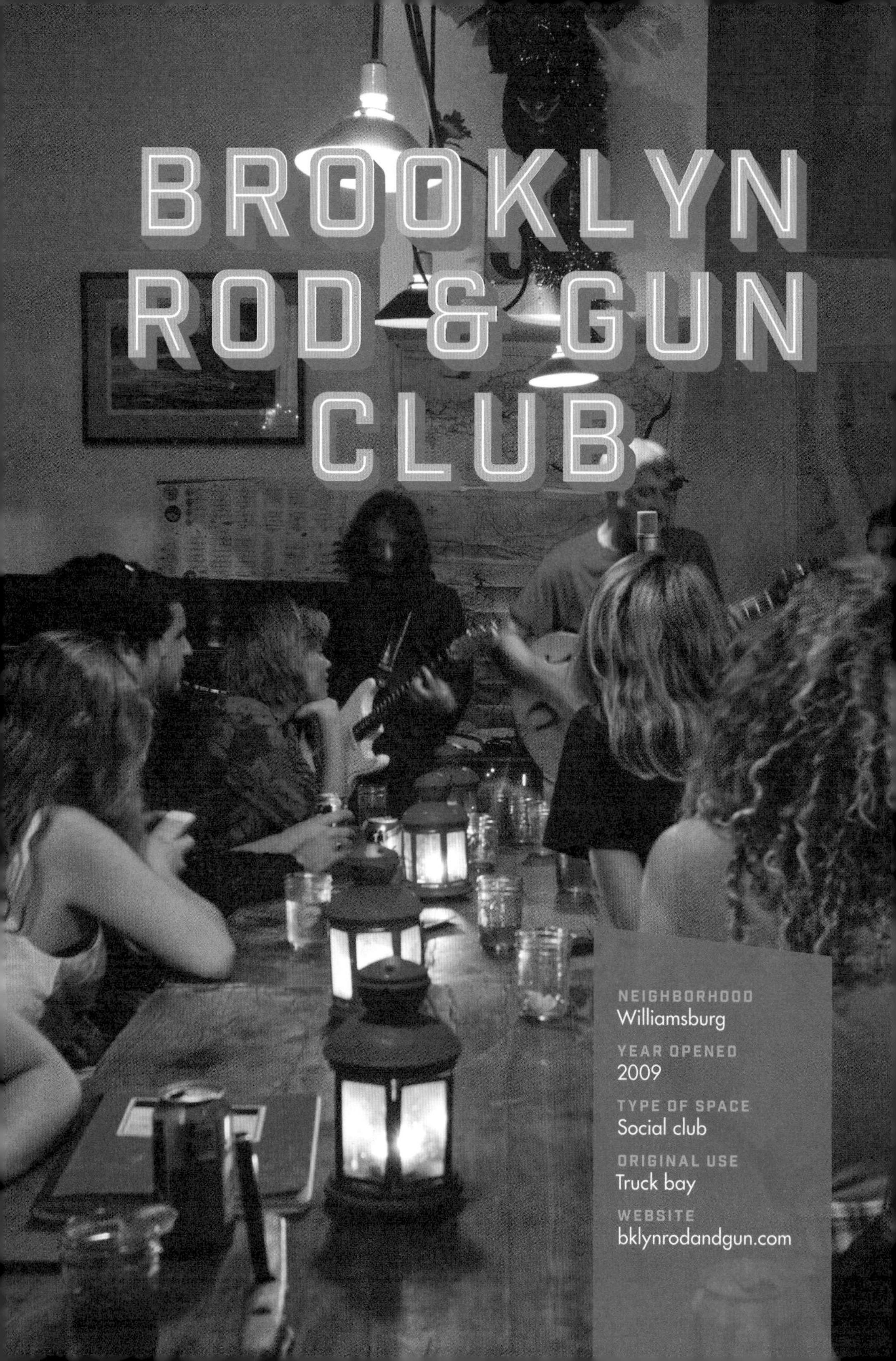

NEIGHBORHOOD
Williamsburg

YEAR OPENED
2009

TYPE OF SPACE
Social club

ORIGINAL USE
Truck bay

WEBSITE
bklynrodandgun.com

**Chris Raymond, who started Brooklyn** Rod & Gun, is that rare city kid who's also an avid outdoorsman. He's an urban New Yorker through and through—born in Park Slope, prep school in the Bronx, college at Pratt, raising his kids in Williamsburg—but he grew up on the waterfront in eastern Queens and learned to fish at an early age. By the time he was in his mid-twenties, he'd played in several bands and was also taking regular fly-fishing trips, so he had the perfect background to start an out-doorsy social club that doubles as a haven for rollicking music performances.

Social clubs have flourished in New York for at least a century, often serving as a gathering place for newly arrived immigrants desperate for a sense of home. In Carroll Gardens there were five different clubs just for people who came from the tiny port city Mola di Bari, and in Bensonhurst there were once clubs sponsored by nearly every town in Southern Italy. Chris was always intrigued by these spots. "They were great neighborhood places that seemed so integral to family and community life," he says. "I watched the neighborhood change and all the social clubs die out, but I always longed for that community hub."

In 2009, opportunity knocked: a friend had a woodworking shop in a former factory on the Williamsburg waterfront, and what had once been the truck bay was about to be vacant. Chris brought in Karl Myers, one of his old bandmates and the owner of high-end instru-ment shop Main Drag Music, and together they opened up the space to emulate an old-fash-ioned sports club. Brooklyn Rod & Gun's stated goal is, in part, "to instill respect, appreciation, and awareness of nature in our urban setting."

"We had weekly meetings with beer and peanuts, we'd watch fishing movies and tell camping stories," Chris says. There were nights spent tying flies together and organizing group hikes.

The Rod & Gun Club, housed in a onetime truck-loading bay, was conceived as a gath-ering place for urban outdoor sportsmen, but took on a second life as a venue for bluesy, folksy, and twangy music.

The club holds regular members-only nights, which vary from surprise intimate performances to small groups of friends trading fishing stories over beers.

In such a tiny space, even a small gathering of foot-stompers can make a show feel packed. During performances, the energy in the room is always electric.

The space also served as a place for other like-minded clubs to meet, like the Appalachian Mountain Club and the North Brooklyn Boat Club before they got their own space (p. 146). Members returning from fishing trips would stop by the club with their catch and fire up the grill. "Some nights twenty people came; others it was just me lying on the table organizing my fishing gear," Chris says. "Either way it was terrific."

Many members are also musicians, and they started hosting drop-in jams and casual shows. "I didn't think the space would be acoustic at all, but it turned out that the angles treat the music in a very sweet way," Chris says. It quickly became clear that $10 one-night memberships add up much faster than annual dues, so the music became much more regular, and all of a type: Roots & Ruckus parties, hootenannies, old-timey jams. "When I was a teenager, everyone was in a punk band; now everyone has a banjo or a ukulele," Chris says. He invites all the strummers in: Brotherhood of the Jug Band Blues, Mor-

gan O'Kane, Old Rugged Sauce, Bloodshot Bill, Alex Battles & the Whiskey Rebellion, and Smokey Hormel have all played often. Loudon Wainwright recorded a secret track, Jon Spencer Blues Explosion played a surprise show, and Les Claypool kicked off the US tour for his twang band there, playing the Primus song "Wynona's Big Brown Beaver"—a song, after all, about fly-fishing—to a standing-room-only crowd.

Now the clubhouse hosts various meetings, band rehearsals, community events, and member nights during the week, and music every weekend. But "this is definitely not a venue," Chris says. "What drives a social club isn't the bottom line; it's about sustaining a community of like-minded people, which I think we've been able to do. The music is great, but nights when there's just a bunch of members sitting around planning a fishing trip over beers—that's magic."

*Photos by Alix and Maximus*

# BUSHWICK CITY FARM

NEIGHBORHOOD
Bushwick

YEAR OPENED
2008, 2011

TYPE OF SPACE
Community garden

ORIGINAL USE
Vacant lot

WEBSITE
bushwickcityfarm.
wordpress.com

**New York City has a long tradition of** guerilla gardening, dating back to the 1970s, when a group of artists calling themselves Green Guerillas threw "seed bombs"—balloons packed with seeds, fertilizer, and water—into abandoned lots in an attempt to combat the Lower East Side's urban decay. The community garden movement flourished in the 1980s; at its peak there were more than 800 patches of reclaimed land across the city planted and tended by neighborhood volunteers, many of which were eventually made permanent by the government. Bushwick City Farm, a huge, lush, volunteer-run oasis in a dense neighborhood with very little green space, is a testament to the strength of guerilla gardening ideals, forty years on: all city dwellers deserve access to green space, and community gardens have the power to bring a neighborhood together.

Food-justice activists Masha Radzinsky and her partner Vinnie Olsen started the first incarnation of the Bushwick City Farm in a vacant lot on Broadway, under the elevated subway line, in the summer of 2008. "The goal was to produce fresh food for the community and to provide food education," says Vinnie, "bringing people back to basics as far as where food comes from and how to grow it responsibly." The tiny green space quickly became a haven, with people of all ages working together to beautify a small bit of their neighborhood. Masha, Vinnie, and many local volunteers kept the farm running for five years, until the owner took back the lot.

On Earth Day 2011, the gardeners began reclaiming a second vacant lot nearby. At 10,000 square feet, the new space is nearly five times as big as the original farm, but it was in far worse condition. Once the site of a gas station, then an apartment building, the lot had been vacant for decades, filling up with garbage and attracting vagrants and drug activity. "The soil was contaminated with a hundred years of building and collapsing and building and collapsing," says Jason Reis, one of the core volunteers. "It was basically a landfill." The group worked for months, fashioning the once-blighted space into a flourishing farm. Eventually the property manager got in touch and requested a proposal to give to the lot's owner. The gardeners were granted permission to stay.

In 2014, the farm has fifty-five raised beds growing more than 100 different vegetables, fruits, herbs, and flowers. A coop made of salvaged wood houses thirty-five chickens, ducks, guinea

The farm grows more than 100 vegetables, fruits, herbs, and flowers. All the planting and harvesting is done by volunteers, as is construction, including more than 50 raised planter beds, a gazebo, and a chicken coop.

hens, and even a turkey that was anonymously left one Thanksgiving. All summer long the farm echoes with the shrieks of children at play, the beat of salsa music, and the hum of lively conversation. The planting, tending, caring, and harvesting is still all done by volunteers, many of whom live in the housing projects surrounding the farm. The entire harvest is given away for free to the community, and people are encouraged to wander in to pull weeds, pick vegetables, or just sit in the shade. Donations meet practical needs: plants and seeds from gardening shops, woodchips from a local landscaping company, pallets from a nearby shipping business.

There's also a small army of neighborhood children who come by daily to plant, build, and learn. "For a kid to see something go from seed to harvest is so cool," says Jason. "And they're more likely to eat what they've grown, so we're planting seeds in a lot of different ways." Evelyn Williams, born and raised in Bed-Stuy, got involved because her eleven-year-old daughter had been spending so much time at the farm, and is now one of the core members of the group. "It was incredible seeing her so excited," Evelyn says. "She's so happy to be part of this."

The farm provides much more than fresh food to the neighborhood. It's a model for self-directed education: volunteers of all ages experience organic gardening, animal care, carpentry, community building, and mutual aid. In an urban environment starved for verdant open space, the farm has also become a great venue for parties, barbecues, and other community events, as well as an informal gathering place for diverse neighbors who might have never spent time together otherwise. "We have a real piece of farm life here," Evelyn says. "It's like having an endless backyard. We all just love it."

*Photos by Alix*

Jason Reis, one of the farm's core volunteers, stakes tomato plants so they grow vertically, making them easier to maintain and eventually harvest.

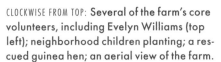

CLOCKWISE FROM TOP: Several of the farm's core volunteers, including Evelyn Williams (top left); neighborhood children planting; a rescued guinea hen; an aerial view of the farm.

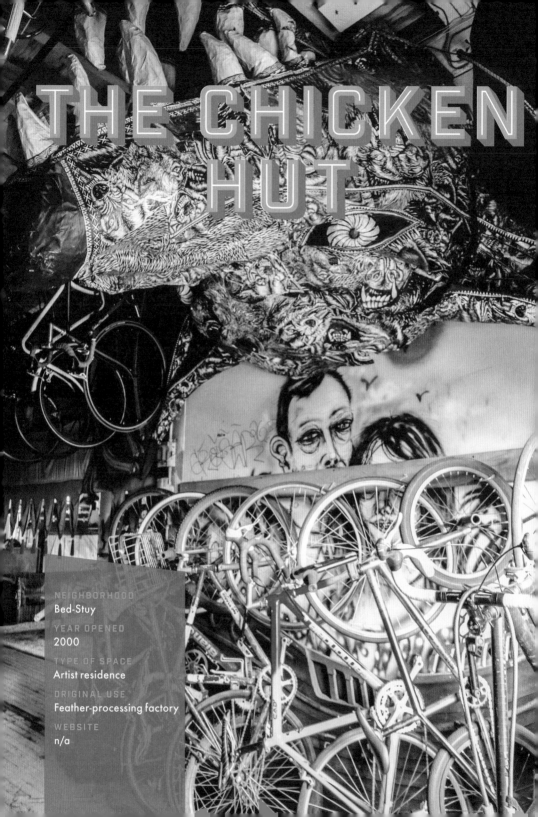

# THE CHICKEN HUT

**NEIGHBORHOOD**
Bed-Stuy

**YEAR OPENED**
2000

**TYPE OF SPACE**
Artist residence

**ORIGINAL USE**
Feather-processing factory

**WEBSITE**
n/a

**In a Brooklyn that gets more sanitized** every day, there are still a few wild holdouts, and the Chicken Hut is one of the last men standing. "This is our reckless abandon studio," says Greg Henderson, who started the space with fellow woodworker JPL in 2000. "It's our home and the place where we can do every crazy fucking thing we've ever thought of."

When Greg and JPL moved in, the building was a feather-processing factory. "The machines would come on, and all these feathers would come puffing up through the floorboards," JPL says. But the empty top floor was an increasingly rare New York City dream: 5,000 square feet of blank space, primed to be sculpted into a manic wonder dreamhouse. "Building out the space was a massive undertaking, and we quickly realized we knew a lot less than we thought," Greg says. They taught themselves plumbing and electrical wiring, and constructed rooms, a woodshop, a bike-building shop, and a kitchen. Often they built until 5 or 6 in the morning,

making myriad trips to the nearby 24-hour hardware store. Incoming roommates were given taped-off "rooms" to build out however they liked. Some put up one wall and then bailed; others formed creative cubbies and stayed for years. The space became a funhouse palimpsest, filled with traces of more than eighty people accumulated over fourteen years.

The Hut has always been home to artists, builders, and renegade makers, from puppeteers to sculptors to luthiers. The space serves as an archive of their creations: robotic aliens, giant rubber sea creatures, and papier-mâché animal heads. It's also a hub for intense artistic collaboration; in 2013 everyone participated in a massive group art show in Long Island City called "Headscapes: A Brainstorm of Installations." Chicken Hut artists built an igloo made of speakers, an enormous metal teepee projecting cartoon letters onto the ceiling, umbrella-cloud sound projectors, and many more indescribable pieces. Over the years the Hut has hosted art

OPPOSITE: The entranceway to the Chicken Hut is filled with dozens of bikes for residents and guests. ABOVE: Greg, Conrad, and JPL, three of the original members of the Chicken Hut, lounge on the roof.

Every room in the Chicken Hut is filled with art, much of it left over from past performances and events. BOTTOM: Some Chicken Hut denizens, including Greg (left), Conrad, and JPL (right)

LEFT: Handmade shelves hold all manner of treasures in the Chicken Hut bedrooms. RIGHT: The Hut's woodworking shop.

salons and open studios to share their work, as well as fundraisers for fellow artists, like prominent street artist Swoon and the art-boat builders Swimming Cities.

And then there are the bikes. Everyone at the Hut rides zealously, and the space is the unofficial clubhouse for the New York chapter of the mutant-bike-building group Black Label Bike Club. In 2002 they hosted the first of what would become an annual freak-bike street party: Bike Kill. "We'd already built the weirdest bikes we could think of," Greg says, "So we decided to have a total day of anarchy to celebrate them." Bike Kill boasts tall bikes, tiny bikes, stacked bikes, bikes with boots for wheels, bikes with steamrollers or surfboards attached, bikes that shoot flames—all arrayed on a Bed-Stuy cul-de-sac for anyone to ride while dodging flung food, foam skeletons, beer cans, and sometimes snow. Hundreds come out for the revelry, especially the finale: tall-bike jousting.

"When we moved in, this area was a wasteland," Greg says. "You could throw burning couches off the roof for an hour and nobody would give a fuck." The massive space was also a perfect place for parties, each event containing many worlds: a dance floor here, a thrash metal band

there, a dirty marionette show down the hall, and a barbecue on the roof—and some six hundred people bouncing back and forth among them. The Hut throws three or four jubilantly anarchic parties a year, filled with a riotous amalgam of people and performers. "The notoriety of this place gave me a name," says Conrad, who performs as DJ Dirtyfinger and has lived at the Hut for a decade. "I started out as the guy who played all the fucking crazy parties here, and now that's all I do."

The Chicken Hut is one of the longest-running underground outposts left in Brooklyn, a boisterous patched-together family that feels increasingly out of place amid all the new condos and buttoned-up populace. It's been legally precarious for fourteen years, but they're in loft-law proceedings; if they win, the building will be brought up to residential code and they'll be granted the right to stay. "If I can't live in this place, there's no way I would stay in this city," says Greg. "New York isn't New York anymore. The grit and character this city is globally renowned for is just gone."

*Photos by Alix and Walter*

The Chicken Hut is the unofficial clubhouse for the New York chapter of the Black Label Bike Club, an international group of mutant-bike builders. Each year since 2002 they've hosted Bike Kill, a daylong freak-bike bonanza celebrating their bizarre two- (or more) wheeled creations.

After Bike Kill, the Chicken Hut hosts a massive all-night party. Performers in 2014 included Faces of Weed and Filthy Savage (pictured above), as well as DJ Dirtyfinger, James Mulry, the Neighbors, American Idle, and many more.

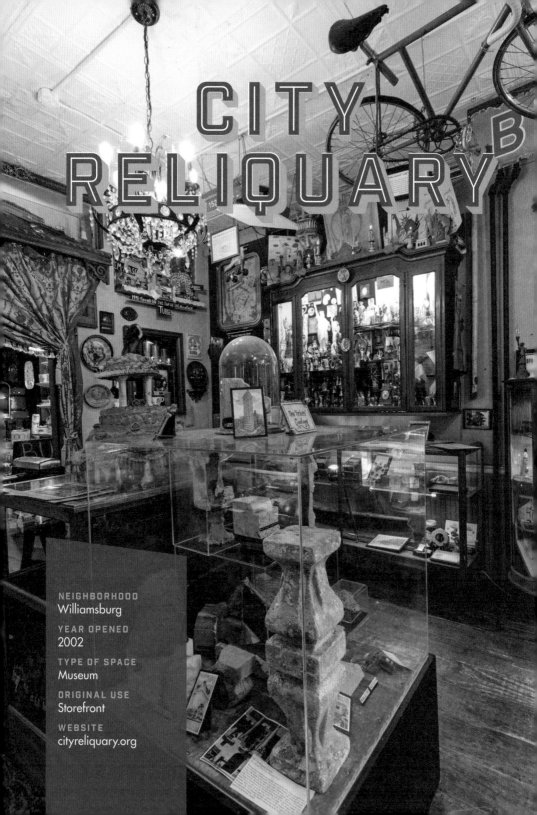

# CITY RELIQUARY

**NEIGHBORHOOD**
Williamsburg

**YEAR OPENED**
2002

**TYPE OF SPACE**
Museum

**ORIGINAL USE**
Storefront

**WEBSITE**
cityreliquary.org

Regularly appearing on lists of New York's hidden gems and quirky attractions, the City Reliquary is a nonprofit micro-museum dedicated to the preservation and appreciation of the city's past by way of its seemingly mundane objects. The Reliquary boasts a densely displayed permanent collection of New York artifacts, as well as a rotating Community Collections gallery showcasing the amassed ephemera of amateur collectors across the city.

The museum began as a tiny window display on the corner of Havemeyer and Grand St. A collector of New York City relics since childhood, Dave Herman decided in 2002 to take advantage of his living room's picture windows to display some of them, such as an irradiated dime from the 1964 World's Fair, a set of dentures found in Dead Horse Bay, and a fire bucket from the Grand Paradise Ballroom across the street, appropriated from a dumpster when the building was converted into lofts in 2001. The window display was accompanied by a push-button audio component that gave a short history of the objects. "I wanted to show respect for the people and the history that came before me, which is sadly kind of uncommon," Dave says. "People show up in a neighborhood and don't think at all about what they've displaced." Dave was thrilled by how many people stopped to interact with the collection: "Anyone could connect with the history of these items, and could feel a sense of ownership."

Like-minded preservationists soon started to get in touch, including Bill Scanga, who had his own micro-museum in his Manhattan studio. Dave soon added a second window display, this one dedicated not to the objects of New York, but to the objects loved by New Yorkers. "It was a way to talk about the character of the city through the obsessions of the people who live here," Dave says. One of the first displays was two of Bill's collections: ET figurines and swung glass. There was a big sidewalk party for the unveiling of the window, complete with food, t-shirts, a piñata, and an alien mascot. Bill continued to work with Dave, and the two put together many more window displays. Then they applied for nonprofit status, amassed a board, and acquired a space for a fully fledged museum in 2006. Many board members contributed artifacts from their personal collections, including relics of historic buildings from an architectural restoration artist, core samples from a geologist, and ephemera from both the 1939 and 1964 World's Fairs. The museum's permanent collection also includes subway tokens, the original 2nd Ave Deli sign, and a Chinatown newsstand called Petrella's Point, on which artist and proprietor Adam Petrella hand-lettered directions to every block in the neighborhood.

The Community Collections turned into a rotating gallery room, which over the years has hosted exhibits on everything from PEZ dispensers to photographs of streetlights to the Embee Sunshade Co, one of Williamsburg's last surviving functional factories. The Reliquary also holds events and block parties, including the annual Bicycle Fetish Day, the Havemeyer Sugar Sweets Festival, movie screenings, music, and a semi-regular Collectors Night, during which people present their own particular passions.

Dave has long since relocated from his Havemeyer St. apartment, and the original window display, like the things that inspired it, has become a tiny bit of New York history that is slowly being forgotten, while everything around it moves on. But the Reliquary has only gained in popularity. "The more Williamsburg changes, the more valuable we are to the neighborhood," Dave asserts.

*Photos by Maximus*

CLOCKWISE FROM TOP LEFT: **Part of the Reliquary's permanent collection; museum cofounders Dave Herman and Bill Scanga; the original sign from the 2nd Ave Deli adorning one Reliquary wall; more of the permanent collection; Lara Jacobs manning the front desk.**

ABOVE: The thriving museum in 2014. BELOW: The picture window where the museum began, which once displayed Dave's personal collection of New York City ephemera.

# CLOUD CITY

NEIGHBORHOOD
Williamsburg

YEAR OPENED
2013

TYPE OF SPACE
Performance venue

ORIGINAL USE
Auto repair shop

WEBSITE
cloudcity.nyc

As with seemingly every building in Williamsburg that isn't a shiny new condo, the space inhabited by Cloud City since 2013 has had many previous artistic incarnations. From 1991 to 1993 the former auto repair shop was the home of Annie Herron's Test-Site, one of the first commercial art galleries in Williamsburg. Over the next few years, it became a hula-hoop studio, then a BDSM club. In 1999 Tanya Gagné, who would go on to open Big Sky Works (p. 20), moved in and started the Trapeze Loft. After she left, the space became a hodgepodge of studios until, at the end of 2012, the six artists who make up the Cloud City collective—Liz Beeby, Nicki Ishmael, Jeff Seal, Andrew Lynch, Katie Melby, and Eric Holm—took over. Before they got there the landlord had gutted the space, so in just three months (and with the help of $10,000 raised on Kickstarter) the group built out six studios, two bathrooms, a kitchen, and a large performance area.

Cloud City is not the collective's first rodeo. From 2007 to 2013, Liz, Nicki, and Jeff lived in and ran the South Williamsburg apartment/venue Dead Herring, in the same repurposed factory that had been home to the first incarnation of Rubulad (p. 172). They hosted music shows in their living room a few times a month, including Chain & the Gang, Reggie Watts, Corn Mo, the Vivian Girls, the Pains of Being Pure at Heart, and the Men. "Dead Herring pretty much made my life in New York," says Nicki. "It gave me something to do and an incredible community to do it in." Toward the end of Dead Herring's run, the collective began adding variety shows and theatrical productions to the mix. When they moved over to Cloud City, gaining a larger space but also noise-sensitive neighbors, they shifted toward more dramatics and less rock.

The varied talents and passions of the collective members inform the events they offer. They've hosted visual art exhibits with IMPOSE magazine, variety shows with alternative comedians like Red Bastard, Butt Kapinski, and ventriloquist Carla Rhodes, and even more unusual fare, like thirty men singing a cappella renditions of Leonard Cohen songs, a chair-pyramid high-wire act, folk operas, original productions, and a bad film festival. "This isn't a cookie-cutter bar, it's not just a corporate venue where people pay too much to get in and then spend too much on drinks," says Jeff. "It's about presenting things we care about, and it isn't about making money. Because we sure as shit don't make any money."

Williamsburg is not getting any easier to make and produce art in. As rents soar, new luxury condos go up at an alarming rate, more and more chain stores push out the remaining small boutiques, and the neighborhood moves further away from art and creativity. "I feel like we belong less and less in this neighborhood," says Liz. "But that also makes me want to dig in even harder." For now, Cloud City remains a venue for experimental, alternative, and reliably high-quality entertainment, and all the collective members are very pleased with their second act. "We're all aware that we're really, really lucky to be doing this," says Nicki.

*Photos by Nicki, Shannon, and Ventiko*

CLOCKWISE FROM TOP: Brave New World Repertory Theatre's 2014 production of Gertrude Stein's *Pink Melon Joy*; Cloud City's founders; the opening night of an *IMPOSE* magazine photo exhibit.

Cloud City hosts many comedy and variety shows, each quirkier and stranger than the last. ABOVE: a live reading of the teleplays of the Halloween episodes of *Night Court* and *Cheers* from 1985 and 1986, an incarnation of the monthly Show & Show Show. INSET: Cloud City members Andrew and Eric leading a stirring singalong of the shows' theme songs.

# CONEY
# ISLAND
# MUSEUM

NEIGHBORHOOD
Coney Island

YEAR OPENED
1985, 1996

TYPE OF SPACE
Museum

ORIGINAL USE
Childs Restaurant

WEBSITE
coneyisland.com

**It's certainly fitting that Dick Zigun,** the unofficial Mayor of Coney Island since 1984, was raised in Bridgeport, CT, where P.T. Barnum was once mayor. "By seven years old I was a Barnum scholar," he says. "I knew that elephants and midgets were patriotic—basically, I was warped at an early age." A flair for pizzazz and an appreciation of the bizarre has served Dick well, making him the perfect spokesman for one of New York City's most fascinating neighborhoods.

Dick moved to Coney Island in 1979 with a master's in theatre from Bennington College. "It was a bizzaro *Warriors* world back then," he says, referring to the cult film about New York street gangs released the very year of his arrival. He started gathering a modest collection of Coney arcana when he could—"I did a lot of trespassing in those days." He also became a regular at some of Coney's stranger attractions, like the World in Wax Musee, which featured a Chamber of Horrors depicting gruesome murder scenes. Lillie Santangelo, who opened the museum with her husband in 1926, was still running the place, and she talked Dick and his friends into helping her put on some shows. "Lillie was totally bats," says Dick. "She was

Grandma Moses on LSD." But the shows were a hit, leading Dick and his friends Costa Mansis and Jane Savitt-Tennen to start the nonprofit arts organization Coney Island USA.

One of the group's most enduring triumphs is the annual Mermaid Parade, "a celebration of ancient mythology and the honky-tonk rituals of the seaside." The first parade took place in 1983, and about 200 people marched—"far more than there were watching," Dick says. But it got a lot of press, which Dick parlayed into a gig doing PR for the Coney Island Chamber of Commerce. "I understand visual communication, and I knew if I wore an antique bathing suit, called myself the Mayor of Coney Island, and got my picture in the paper, people would pay attention." They did. The Mermaid Parade has become the largest art parade in the country; in 2014 close to 800,000 people attended and 5,000 marched. "Now there's a whole generation that's never known New York without the Mermaid Parade," Dick says. "It's just the way New York City celebrates summer. So I invented a holiday, which is a dream come true."

Dick created much more than a holiday—he's built a legacy of Coney Island promotion and preservation. Coney Island USA is now a multi-

The Coney Island Sideshow features a traditional "10 in 1" continuous performance, with 10 acts each hour. The 2014 season included fire breathing, contortion, sword swallowing, and a lot more.

Sideshow performers help an audience member stand on the strongman's "bed of nails."

arts center running a vast array of programming, at the forefront of which is the Coney Island Museum, opened in 1985 in the building where Nathan's Famous Hot Dogs now stands. A decade later Dick moved it a few blocks down the boardwalk, into a building as historically rich as the collection it houses: built in 1917, it was home to the first of Coney's two Childs Restaurants, then a casino, a circus sideshow, and a pinball arcade. Coney Island USA took over in 1996, bought the building in 2007, and fought successfully for it to be given National Landmark status in 2010. The museum features a wonderful array of Coney history, including funhouse mirrors (great for selfies!), old bumper cars, and a scale model of the original 1903 Luna Park.

Then there's the Coney Island Circus Sideshow, the last surviving "10 in 1"—ten different acts each hour, from sword swallowing to contortion to glass walking. Coney Island USA has also held Burlesque at the Beach since the late 1980s, starting with Wildgirl's weekly Go-Go-Rama. Burlesque stars like Dirty Martini, Bambi the Mermaid, and Julia Atlas Muz cut their teeth on the boardwalk, and Jo "Boobs" Weldon launched the School of Burlesque there in 2003. There's a Sideshow School as well, where anyone can learn to spit fire or hammer nails into various orifices. "It's our own fault sideshow and burlesque got so popular," Dick says. "We're the ones teaching people how to compete with us!" With the Coney Island Film Society, the annual Congress of Curious Peoples, the Coney Island Tattoo and Motorcycles Convention, the interactive Halloween play Creepshow at the Freakshow, and more, Dick's programming is as beautiful and bizarre as Coney Island itself.

*Photos by Remi*

CLOCKWISE FROM TOP: **Dick Zigun, unofficial Mayor of Coney Island since 1984 and founder of Coney Island USA in 1980; an audience awaiting the start of the sideshow; Coney Island USA's landmarked 1917 building; bumper cars and more in the Coney Island Museum.**

# DEATH BY AUDIO

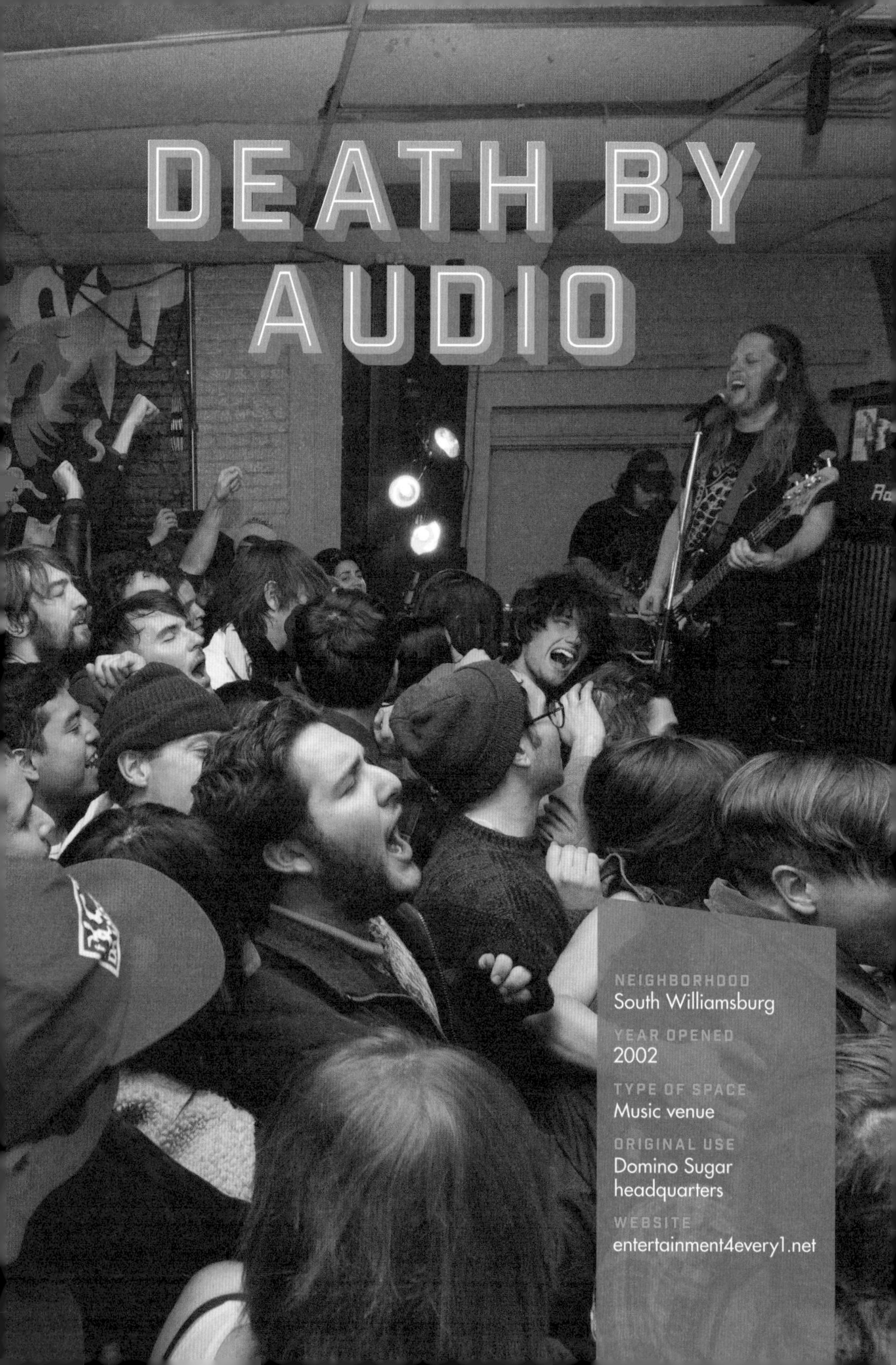

NEIGHBORHOOD
South Williamsburg

YEAR OPENED
2002

TYPE OF SPACE
Music venue

ORIGINAL USE
Domino Sugar
headquarters

WEBSITE
entertainment4every1.net

**Death By Audio is one of the last vanguards** of the wild music scene that careened through Williamsburg in the 1990s and 2000s. Dozens of influential DIY venues have come and gone—ParisLondonNewYorkWestNile, Glass House Gallery, Mighty Robot, Monster Island, and 285 Kent, to name just a few—most within a few blocks of where Death By Audio continues to put on noisy, sweaty, raucous all-ages shows nearly every night. The walls teem with murals by more than a dozen Brooklyn artists, and the space is dotted with independent videogame consoles built by the Babycastles collective. More than 1,000 bands come through each year, and 2011 holds the record for the most acts: 1,163.

The space was started by Oliver Ackermann, frontman of the noise rock band A Place to Bury Strangers, as an electronics workshop. Oliver had been constructing handmade custom guitar effects pedals since 1999—he specializes in distortion, and his pedals have names like Soundwave Breakdown, Apocalypse, and Supersonic Fuzz Gun. In 2002 he moved into the South Williamsburg building that once housed the Domino Sugar headquarters, bringing his Death By Audio operation with him. He eventually built out the space to encompass his company factory and headquarters, a recording studio, a record label, and the 150-capacity venue. Over the years his pedals have been used by the likes of Trent Reznor, Jeff Tweedy, and U2's The Edge. He's picked up collaborators along the way, including his business partner Matt Conboy and DBA's booker and sound engineer, Edan Wilber, who cut his teeth working for Brooklyn's DIY music king, Todd P (see Trans-Pecos, p. 208). The space became a nonprofit in 2009.

Now DBA's musical focus reflects Edan's wide-ranging tastes. "I'm there every single night running sound," he says, "so it's got to be something that's interesting to me, something that can hold my attention after the thousands of performances I've seen." The music tends to be loud, with permutations on noise rock, heavy rock, pop rock, metal, and experimental or harsh noise. "If it sounds awesome, and if I think it's going to be cool live, we put it on," he says. Some of the bigger acts to come through have been Dirty Projectors, Thurston Moore, Pissed Jeans, Future Islands, Thee Oh Sees, Paint It Black, Suuns, Universal Order of Armeggadon, and Ty Segall.

The Brooklyn underground music scene is a tight-knit group, and Death By Audio, which is known for consistently high quality music and that intense, intimate, but low-pressure atmosphere that marks an underground venue, is well respected and supported. "The DIY movement in Brooklyn has easily been the most important thing in my life up to this point," says Edan. "I've never felt such an amazing sense of creative community."

But as Williamsburg continues its march toward hyper-gentrification, the future of small, scrappy spaces becomes ever more precarious. "Death By Audio and Glasslands and so many other spots, we've helped make Williamsburg safe and interesting," Edan says. "But I'm starting to feel like I'm clinging to something that's slipping through my fingers."

*Photos by Walter*

A sampling of DBA's musical fare and raucous crowds. PREVIOUS SPREAD: Natural Child. THIS PAGE, CLOCKWISE FROM TOP LEFT: Black Pus; Ty Segall; Downtown Boys; Chat Logs.

CLOCKWISE FROM TOP: A Halloween party in the back of the space, normally not open to the public; Yukary of the ZZZ's; Ryo Inoue.

# FIREHOUSE SPACE

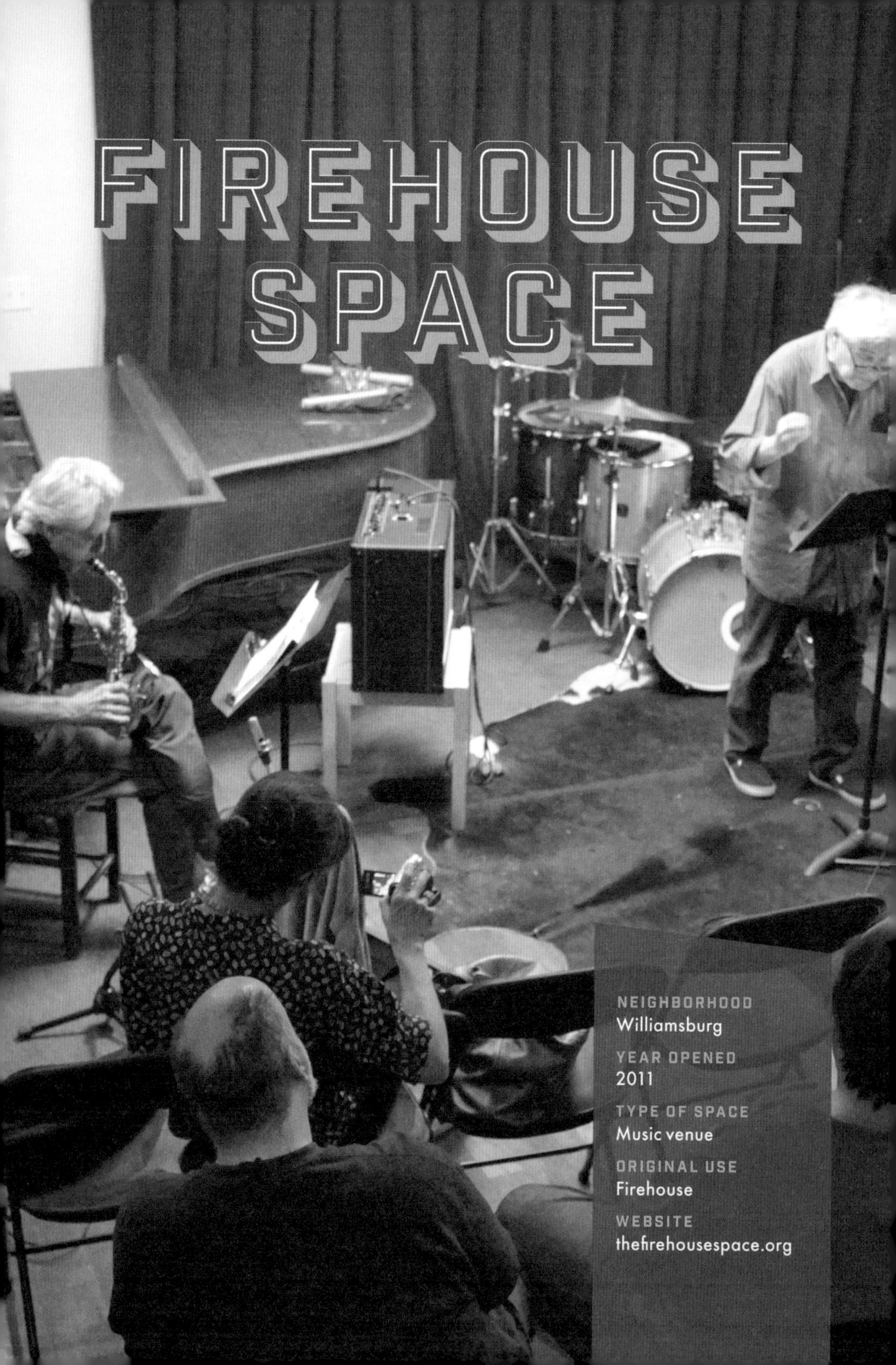

NEIGHBORHOOD
Williamsburg

YEAR OPENED
2011

TYPE OF SPACE
Music venue

ORIGINAL USE
Firehouse

WEBSITE
thefirehousespace.org

**Behind the unassuming façade of a** decommissioned nineteenth-century firehouse is a performance venue featuring a wide range of creative jazz, free improvisation, and experimental and contemporary classical music. It's also a stunning living space, inhabited by classically trained composer and pianist Sandra Sprecher, her two sons, and their two dogs.

As the director of the Firehouse Space, Sandra coordinates programming four days per week. What the performances all have in common, she says, is that they all make for "challenging listening." "These are performance virtuosos who can do improvisation, who champion new music; they're these new animals doing things on their instruments that you never thought possible."

The space opened as a venue in September 2011. Many luminaries of the genre have come through, including improvising pianist Connie Crothers, the Kaufman Center's alt-classical youth ensemble Face the Music, internationally renowned creator of soundpainting Walter Thompson, chamber quartet Yarn/Wire, avant-garde violin duo String Noise, perfor-

mance-art operas from Panoply Performance Lab, dissective minimalists Ensemble Pamplemousse, and experimental classical musicians Iktus Percussion.

The versatile space can be configured in different ways to suit the different types of performance. There are stages on both floors, and Sandra has experimented with multi-level performances, having musicians on both floors as well as some on the spiral staircase. The space has also been used for weddings, photo shoots, and other events. By coincidence (or because, well, this is Brooklyn), Sandra's next-door neighbor is a production engineer, so musicians sometimes record albums and live sessions there as well.

"The best part of running a space like this is having these amazing concerts right in my own house," Sandra says. "As a composer, my ears are always wide open, so it's thoroughly exciting to run this space."

*Photos by Jeff and Maximus*

OPPOSITE: **Steve Dalachinsky reading poetry and Rocco John Iacovone on alto saxophone.**
ABOVE: **Matt Lavelle leads his 12 House Orchestra.**

CLOCKWISE FROM TOP: The Firehouse's exterior, featuring its original doors; the Eslabon Art House Performance Salon; art on display; Ras Moshe Unit; Veterans of Free All-Star Ensemble.

CLOCKWISE FROM TOP: **12 House Orchestra;**
Ken Filiano; the Eslabon Salon.

FIVEMYLES

NEIGHBORHOOD
Crown Heights

YEAR OPENED
1999

TYPE OF SPACE
Art gallery

ORIGINAL USE
Garage

WEBSITE
fivemyles.org

"**Everybody in the neighborhood knows, if** you need something, come to FiveMyles," says Hanne Tierney, founder and artistic director of the Crown Heights gallery, performance venue, and community gathering space.

Hanne opened the 1,500-square-foot nonprofit gallery, which is dedicated to showcasing the work of emerging, under-represented, and minority artists, in a former garage in 1999. No stranger to the New York art world, Hanne has been writing and performing avant-garde puppet shows and reinterpreted plays since 1980, gracing stages at the Whitney Museum, the Guggenheim, BAM, Franklin Furnace, and many more cultural venues. FiveMyles was originally intended to be a studio for both Hanne and her son Myles, an AP journalist who was then in East Africa working on a documentary for the Human Rights Commission that focused on incarcerated former child soldiers. Tragically, Myles was killed in Sierra Leone in 1999.

"It was supposed to be his space," Hanne says. "So we decided to make it into something joyous in his honor." She has worked tirelessly ever since to create an inviting and well-integrated performance and exhibition space, one that is both respected by the art world and accessible to the diverse Crown Heights community.

FiveMyles presents six formal exhibitions each year, and close to half the artists shown are African American. "We've always stood with Africa, East Africa in particular; that is my son's legacy," Hanne says. "And it's very exciting for the kids in the neighborhood to see contemporary work from Africa." Hanne also works to bring East African art to an even larger audience. In 2004 she brought 150 pieces of contemporary Kenyan art to the States for five different galleries, including the Brooklyn Public Library, Long Island University's Salena Gallery, and galleries in Red Hook and Bed-Stuy. She has also coordinated African artists-in-residence

OPPOSITE: A Crown Heights troupe dancing against a backdrop painted by Matt Freedman, with help from friends and neighbors. ABOVE: Sculpture, photographs, and drawings from the exhibit "Unframed," summer 2014.

at FiveMyles and helped to draw them into the New York art world. In one instance, Kenyan artist James Mbuthia constructed a chicken coop installation, and prominent Brooklyn artists were invited to create chickens to put in it.

During the summer, FiveMyles runs the Space-Program, turning the gallery over, free of charge, to young and emerging artists and musicians. They then curate art shows, music and dance performances, poetry readings, film screenings, and the St. John's Place On Stage performance festival, which has taken place annually since 2000.

Watching the upheaval caused by the accelerated gentrification in Crown Heights over the last decade has been difficult for Hanne. "When I first came here, this sidewalk would be filled up and down with kids playing," she says. "The girls were double-dutching, the guys were playing dominoes, everyone was outside. But now it's empty. So much of our community has disappeared." Back in 2008 she curated a sound and video installation at FiveMyles called "There Goes the Neighborhood," featuring recordings of Crown Heights residents discussing the fear of losing their homes and community, over a silent looped video of new condominium construction. "It was the most painful exhibition we ever had," Hanne says.

In 2015 a 172-unit luxury condo will open two doors down from FiveMyles, which Hanne fears could mark the end of the community. But she continues to fight for her neighbors: screening documentaries, hosting talks, writing letters to Al-

FiveMyles is a true community space for people in the neighborhood. After concerts and events, Hanne leaves chairs out so that people can gather and spend time together well into the night.

bany about police harassment, sending people to the Crown Heights Tenant Union if they come to her with tales of abusive landlords, and, of course, curating more and more exhibits, showing the work of more and more artists. "Hanne is so important to this community," says Francelle Jones, a photographer whose work has been featured in the gallery. "She brings people together, and she allows people who have lived in this neighborhood to feel as though they're still a part of something. That is so important."

*Photos by Hanne and Maximus*

CLOCKWISE FROM TOP: "Art/Sewn," curated by Ward Mintz; Yoshiko Chuma and the School of Hard Knocks; DJ Speedy spins at the opening of Sam Tufnell's sculpture show; Friends and neighbors on a summer afternoon; Hanne Tierney (center) with collaborators and community members.

# FLUX FACTORY

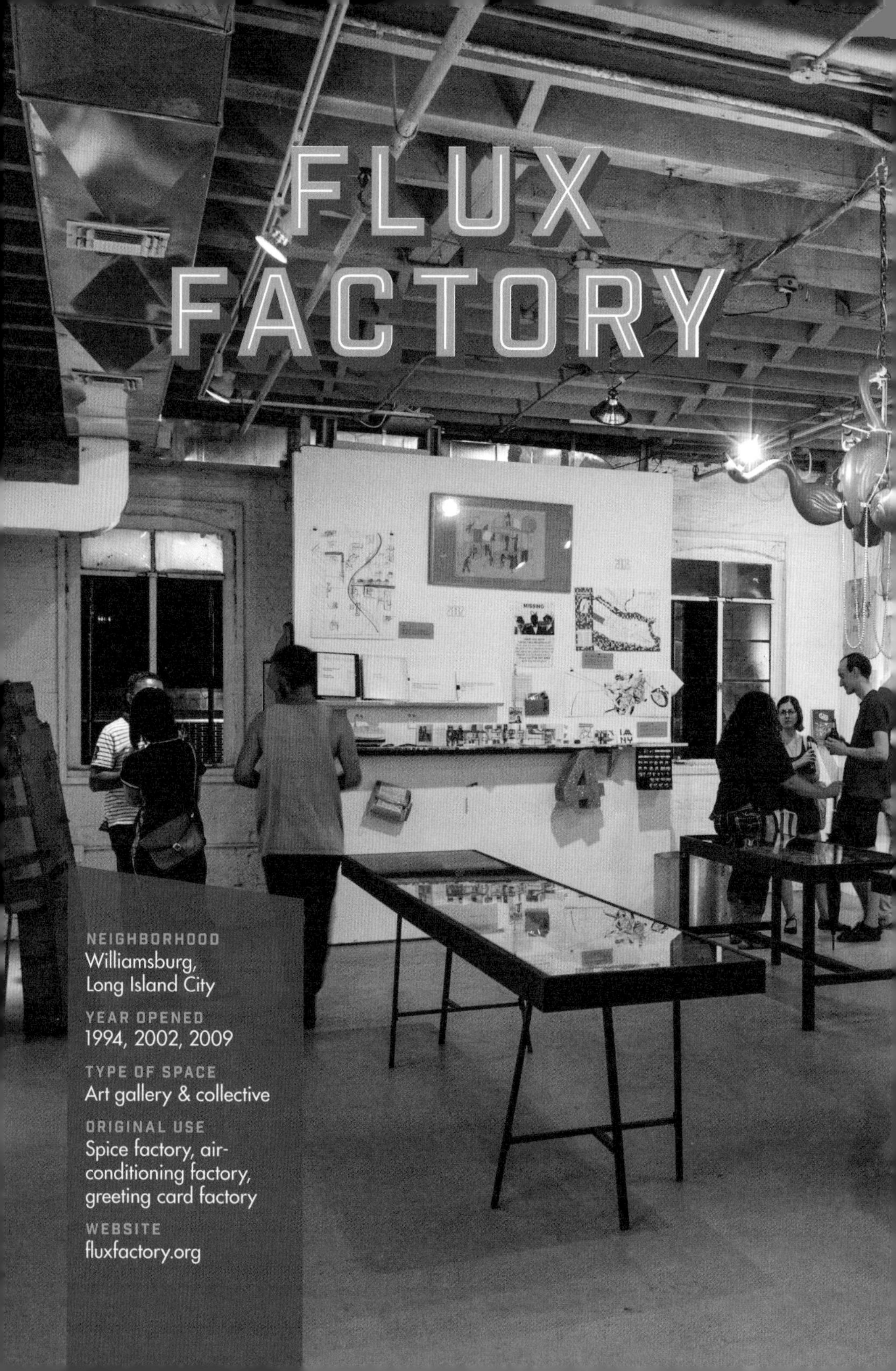

**NEIGHBORHOOD**
Williamsburg,
Long Island City

**YEAR OPENED**
1994, 2002, 2009

**TYPE OF SPACE**
Art gallery & collective

**ORIGINAL USE**
Spice factory, air-
conditioning factory,
greeting card factory

**WEBSITE**
fluxfactory.org

"**The sense of playfulness at Flux is** unparalleled," says Flux Factory member Georgia Muenster. Adds Adrian Owen, "But we're professional as well. We have the heads behind all these crazy things we do." Flux has perfected that balance over twenty years: it's one of the largest and longest-running arts groups in New York City. The group's focus is on collaboration, extreme creativity, and a jubilant sense of silliness that often leads to serious critical engagement.

Flux is in many ways the doyenne of Brooklyn's vibrant underground art scene. It has inhabited three spaces in two boroughs; hundreds of artists have lived, collaborated, and exhibited within its many walls. The first Flux was started in 1994 by Morgan Meis and several other New School undergrads in a former spice factory on the Williamsburg waterfront—the same building that would later become Monster Island, where Secret Project Robot (p. 182) and Todd P (p. 208) got their starts. In 1998 Flux became a nonprofit, and by 2002 they had been priced out of Williamsburg and decamped for Long Island City, Queens. The Fluxers signed a fifteen-year lease on a former air-conditioning factory, only to have the MTA kick them out six years later under the eminent domain mandate, in order to build a Grand Central Terminal rail link. Undeterred, the Fluxers opened their third incarnation a dozen blocks west in 2009, in a three-floor, 7,500-square-foot former greeting card factory, which they divided into fourteen art studios, workshops and exhibition spaces, and a rooftop garden. The main gallery still has one of the factory's original industrial conveyor belts, put to use in various exhibits.

The Fluxers—fourteen artists at a time, plus four staff members and a few artists-in-residence— do a *lot* with that space. Each year Flux holds around seventy events, including visual art shows, installations, performances, potluck presentations, screenings, workshops, and lectures. "The thing that's compelling to me about the whirlwind of multidisciplinary works being created, displayed, and destroyed here is not the work

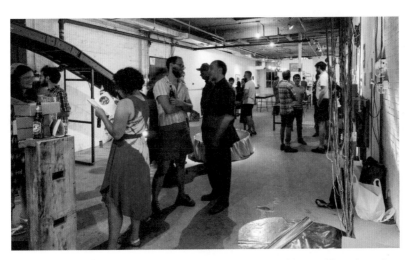

Flux was one of the longest-running art collectives in Brooklyn—although it relocated to Queens in 2002. OPPOSITE AND ABOVE: In August 2014 the nonprofit celebrated its 20th anniversary with an exhibition called "Homecoming," displaying bits and pieces from two decades of innovative, collaborative, and extremely playful work.

itself—it's the completely different mode of relations," says Nat Roe, Flux's Executive Director.

Everything at Flux happens, per their mission statement, with a "rigorous commitment to the collaborative process." There are four major thematic group shows each year, involving art, performance, and community events, and the main gallery is completely transformed for each. It has been an enormous cabinet of curiosities, a giant music box, an interactive game show, a Rube Goldberg machine, a performance art bazaar, a city for cats, a sleep factory, and a Caribbean carnival, among many other incarnations. Collective-wide shows are frenetic yet incredibly thoughtful, extremely ambitious as well as rambunctiously gleeful. "There's really no context for this sort of stuff in mainstream culture," says Jason Eppink.

The hundreds of artists who have cycled through have presented a spectrum of specialties, like crafting autonomous zones, weaving holographic images, studying waste as a cultural construct, assembling collective realities, and examining the thresholds of form and perception. Many have exhibited internationally and won myriad art awards and grants, and all display some sort of "Fluxiness," the ineffable quality inherent to what Flux is all about. "It's the thing it takes for someone to endure being part of this crazy mess," says Douglas Paulson. Christina Vassallo, the former Executive Director, adds, "Fluxiness is constantly changing, based on who's here. You know it when you see it, though. It's a state of mind."

*Photos by Maximus*

CLOCKWISE FROM TOP LEFT: A collective member's music studio; a detail of the massive "Exquisite Contraption," a collaboratively conceived and constructed Rube Goldberg machine spanning the whole building; glass art on display.

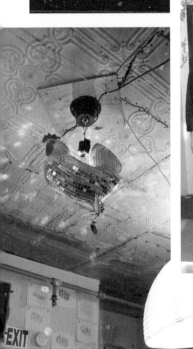

CLOCKWISE FROM TOP LEFT: **The original conveyor belt leftover from the space's past as a greeting card factory; Flux's woodshop, one of many collaborative workspaces; a group of Fluxers; a chicken disco ball in the kitchen.**

# FREECANDY

NEIGHBORHOOD
Clinton Hill

YEAR OPENED
2009

TYPE OF SPACE
Art gallery &
coworking space

ORIGINAL USE
Parking garage

WEBSITE
freecandy.tv

**Todd Triplett, founder of mixed-use art,** coworking, and music venue Freecandy Creative Space, got off to a rough start. In 2007, he and two business partners invested $1.2 million to create a music venue in a derelict former liquor store in Downtown Brooklyn. Construction was finished, all the permits and licenses squared away when, four weeks from opening, the Department of City Planning swooped in to reclaim the building under the eminent domain mandate: the space would be demolished to make room for a thirty-story condo. Todd and his partners, who had never been told that this was a possibility, lost everything, pushed out of business before they even began.

Incredibly, Todd kept his dream of opening an art space alive. By 2009 he'd found a new location—a 7,000-square-foot 1920s parking garage—and was ready to try again. This time he decided to try crowdfunding with Kickstarter, a platform that had recently launched. "I was probably one of the first 100 people to use it," he says. The campaign was a success—Todd raised more than $20,000, and Freecandy was born.

A few years into its stride, Freecandy has become a malleable space for independent creative individuals to convene and showcase their work. By day it's used for coworking, with creative types building apps, mixing music, managing bands, and designing streetwear; by night the space morphs into an art gallery, music venue, black-box theatre, or whatever the situation calls for. Todd's goal is for Freecandy to be a hub of creativity and community, bringing all different kinds of people together in what he calls "directed serendipity" to see what develops.

The name of the space means a lot of things to Todd. For one, it references the lesson we're taught as children: don't take candy from strangers. "Why not?" Todd asks. "I get it, there are pedophiles and whatnot, but most of the time, when someone offers you candy, it's from the kindness of their heart." Todd also thinks of his space as something of a confectionary, "creating something sweet for the world." And because the focus is on emerging artists, he says, "We're developing what we hope will be the next big sweet thing."

Freecandy has hosted events such as the Hillstock and AfroPunk festivals and concerts ranging from the Japanese post-punk trio ZZZs to Australian neo-soul quartet Hiatus Kaiyote. When the predominantly black and queer collective HOWDOYOUSAYYAMINAFRICAN withdrew from the 2014 Whitney Biennial, they brought their troupe over to Freecandy for an explosive, raucous evening of spoken word, hip-hop, performance art, dance, film, and song.

Todd, whose grandfather was a jazz musician, believes that art and music have the power to change the world, and he wants Freecandy to carry on the cultural legacy of Bed-Stuy, Clinton Hill, and Ft. Greene. One of his proudest moments was when Spike Lee turned up for an event and said that Freecandy reminded him of Paradise Garage, the legendary New York dance club from the 1970s and '80s. "The vibe of this place, the bones, it's just so authentic," Todd says. "It's exactly what I envisioned when I was moving to New York."

*Photos by Alix*

Walking into Freecandy, the building's previous life as a parking garage is apparent in the inclined concrete entryway. Once filled with the sound of car horns and the smell of exhaust, it has been decorated with murals and remade into an inviting creative space.

Freecandy's evening fare ranges from mixers to readings to music performances, with many cutting-edge artists coming through.

During the day, Freecandy is used for coworking and what founder Todd Triplett calls "directed serendipity": creative people congregating, sharing ideas, and collaborating.

# GALAPAGOS
# ART SPACE

**NEIGHBORHOOD**
Williamsburg, Dumbo

**YEAR OPENED**
1995, 2006

**TYPE OF SPACE**
Performance venue

**ORIGINAL USE**
Mayonnaise factory,
horse stable

**WEBSITE**
galapagosartspace.com

**The *grande dame* of Brooklyn's alternative** arts venues, Galapagos has been championing the borough's emerging, experimental, eclectic, and extraordinary performers since 1995. "My vision is for Galapagos to present the best in many disciplines, and for it to be a place for cross-pollination," says founder Robert Elmes. "The more lines you cross, the more groups you weave together, the stronger the rope will be."

Robert, a sculptor from a small town near Vancouver, moved to Greenpoint in 1989 and joined up with a small, ambitious contingent of artists inspired by Williamsburg's derelict landscape and nascent art scene. He was involved with the early-1990s Immersionist spectacles Cats Head, Flytrap, and Organism, interactive nightlong happenings in derelict warehouses filled with installations and performances. In 1993 Robert and five other artists rented the Old Dutch Mustard Factory on Metropolitan Avenue, by the waterfront—at $1,200 per month

for the entire five-story building—and set about putting on huge monthly extravaganzas. For one show they built waterfalls inside the factory; for another they installed 500 candles in the walls as a backdrop for an elaborate cabaret.

In 1995 Robert signed a ten-year lease for a former mayonnaise factory on then-desolate North 6th Street. Galapagos was the first venue of its kind in Williamsburg, and it quickly became lauded as a pioneering arts incubator. Most bills featured several kinds of performances, mixing audiences and exposing people to radical new work, including experimental theatre, avant-garde dance, hybrid movement pieces, improvised short plays, outré puppet shows, campy cabaret, and more. Musical performers included St. Etienne, the Scissor Sisters, and Fischerspooner. Donal O'Ceilleachair's highly respected experimental film night Ocularis ran for years. The Phat Tuesday alt-performance series helped launch careers of burlesque stars

OPPOSITE: Burlesque performance by Madame Rosebud during the monthly Floating Kabarette variety show. ABOVE: The nightlife sensation Dances of Vice, a regular event at Galapagos, here with a Swan Lake–themed fashion show.

like Julia Atlas Muz and the World Famous *BOB*. Book agent-turned-humorist John Hodgman hosted the Little Gray Books lecture series, with guests like Elizabeth Gilbert, Chuck Klosterman, and David Rees. At a time when Williamsburg was becoming known internationally for fostering a performance scene of dizzying range, Galapagos was at its helm.

But by 2006, when Galapagos' lease was up, Williamsburg had become a drastically different place, and Galapagos was facing an astronomical rent increase. Robert was making plans to move the operation to Berlin when real-estate developer David Walentas, whose Two Trees

Management owns much of the Dumbo neighborhood, offered him twice the space for half the price if he brought Galapagos there. "Two Trees were very helpful, and it was clear they were putting art and culture in the center of their development plans," Robert says. And he was interested in pursuing what a more sophisticated, grown-up Galapagos would look like.

Galapagos moved into a 9,000-square-foot 1905 horse stable, one of New York City's first LEED-certified venues. The programming in the Dumbo space is indeed more sophisticated but no less eclectic, showcasing emerging stars in cabaret, burlesque, opera, fashion, and dance.

In its original Williamsburg location, Galapagos had a shallow pond in the vestibule, and art pieces were hung above it, reflected in its depths. In the "grown-up" Galapagos in Dumbo, there is a much fancier lake: 1,600 square feet, snaking underneath the mezzanine seating.

LEFT: Dances of Vice's Alice in Wonderland Ball, complete with Red and White Queens. TOP RIGHT: A performance of Swan Lake by Company XIV. BOTTOM RIGHT: "The Birthday Show" hosted by party organizers and Galapagos regulars the Love Show.

Some successful series include the weekly circus and burlesque variety show Floating Kabarette ("That show alone puts probably $40 million into the performing arts community each year," Robert says), the Nerd Nite eclectic lecture series, Get Smart's TED-style talks interspersed with cabaret acts, the Wonder Show's magicians, and the Creative Mornings talks. The venue is more beloved than ever, drawing international talent and audiences alike.

Since it opened in 1995, Galapagos has always been completely audience supported, never taking grants or government money. The space has achieved great success in two of Brooklyn's most distinguished artistic neighborhoods, and its impact on New York's cultural landscape would be difficult to overstate.

*Photos by Alix and Michael*

# GEMINI & SCORPIO

NEIGHBORHOOD
Gowanus

YEAR OPENED
2011

TYPE OF SPACE
Party & performance
venue

ORIGINAL USE
Industrial woodshop

WEBSITE
geminiandscorpio.com

**When Larisa Fuchs (aka Miss Scorpio) met** Jamie Kiffel-Alcheh (aka Miss Gemini) in 2002, the two bonded over online dating. "It was not very accepted back then," Larisa says. "But we wanted people to know how great it was." The two started curating an email list of interesting things to do with your online paramour, "so that even if the date was boring, you'd still have fun." That led to throwing "singles parties that don't suck," with themes, costumes, and a variety of unusual entertainment. "We started with a Valentine's Day party, then Halloween, then New Year's, and suddenly it was my full-time job," Larisa says. After Jamie decamped for Los Angeles, Larisa continued creating wild shindigs, which have steadily gotten bigger, more lavish, and more daring.

Larisa has produced Gemini & Scorpio events at Lincoln Center, Spiegeltent, Bell House, Irondale Center, Galapagos Art Space (p. 82), a Russian banya, and the *Queen of Hearts*, a Mississippi-style paddleboat. The costume-required fêtes have beautifully strange and evocative names, like the Vault of Golden Vapors, Cantina at the End of the Universe, Speakeasy Dollhouse, the Drowned Ball, and Masquerade Macabre. "A Gemini & Scorpio party isn't one you drop into casually on your way to something else," Larisa says. "Our guests leave the house knowing they're coming to see us, dress to the theme, and stay with us all night."

To keep everyone titillated, the soirées feature a smorgasbord of entertainment: aerialists, contortionists, burlesque and belly dancers, body painters, fire spinners, and fortune tellers—and those are just the easy ones to explain. Spectacles have also included toy piano mayhem, Victorian music box mix, carnival games made of marshmallows, a handmade contraption orchestra, an all-female AfroBrazilian drumming group, and space music made with beatboxing, a theremin, and a bike wheel. Larisa brings numerous performers back again and again, and she has helped launch many a creative career. "Sometimes I take on artists as a personal cause and keep booking them until people realize how incredible they are," she says.

OPPOSITE: Batala NYC, an all-female AfroBrazilian samba reggae drumming band, playing at the Mermaid Parade afterparty, Sea Creature Stomp. ABOVE: Dolly Debutante performing with Professor Cunningham and His Old School at Swing House, a regular 1920s speakeasy party.

After years of being nomadic, in 2011 Larisa found a permanent base for Gemini & Scorpio in a semi-derelict industrial woodshop. It took a year, all her savings, and a $32,000 Kickstarter campaign to get the space into serviceable shape: major structural repairs to the rotted floor and ceiling, new windows, walls, bathrooms, insulation, and electrical system. In addition to lavish parties, the new space allows Larisa to host "all the calmer, wonderful things that support my creative community," she says. There have been lectures on sex in the dictionary, the art of trespassing, and the history of heavy metal, plus storytelling events, swing dancing classes, clothing swaps, clandestine cabarets, a one-man steampunk musical, and multi-week immersive theatrical shows, just to name a few.

And she never stopped curating that events list, which now has thousands of subscribers and is one of the most important resources for quirky and colorful things to do in NYC. She's absolutely committed to sending it out every Friday, no matter where she is—Paris, the Edinburgh Fringe Festival, even once in a car on the way to Burning Man. "I consider it my community service," she says. "It's a way for me to give back to the people who trust me and honor me with their presence at my events."

*Photos by Andrew, Linus, Maximus, and Tod*

LEFT: Founder Larisa Fuchs (right) and Kiana Love leading the blessing ceremony at the Gemini & Scorpio Loft Launch in December 2013. RIGHT: Human statue Galatea at an afterparty for an immersive production of *A Midsummer Night's Dream.*

CLOCKWISE FROM TOP: Belly-dancer Paige Stevenson performing at Fairy Forest Frolic; alien monster puppet funk band BIG NAZO during Cantina at the End of the Universe, an annual Star Wars sci-fi mashup celebration; burlesque dancers Angela Harriell and David Slone of the Love Show.

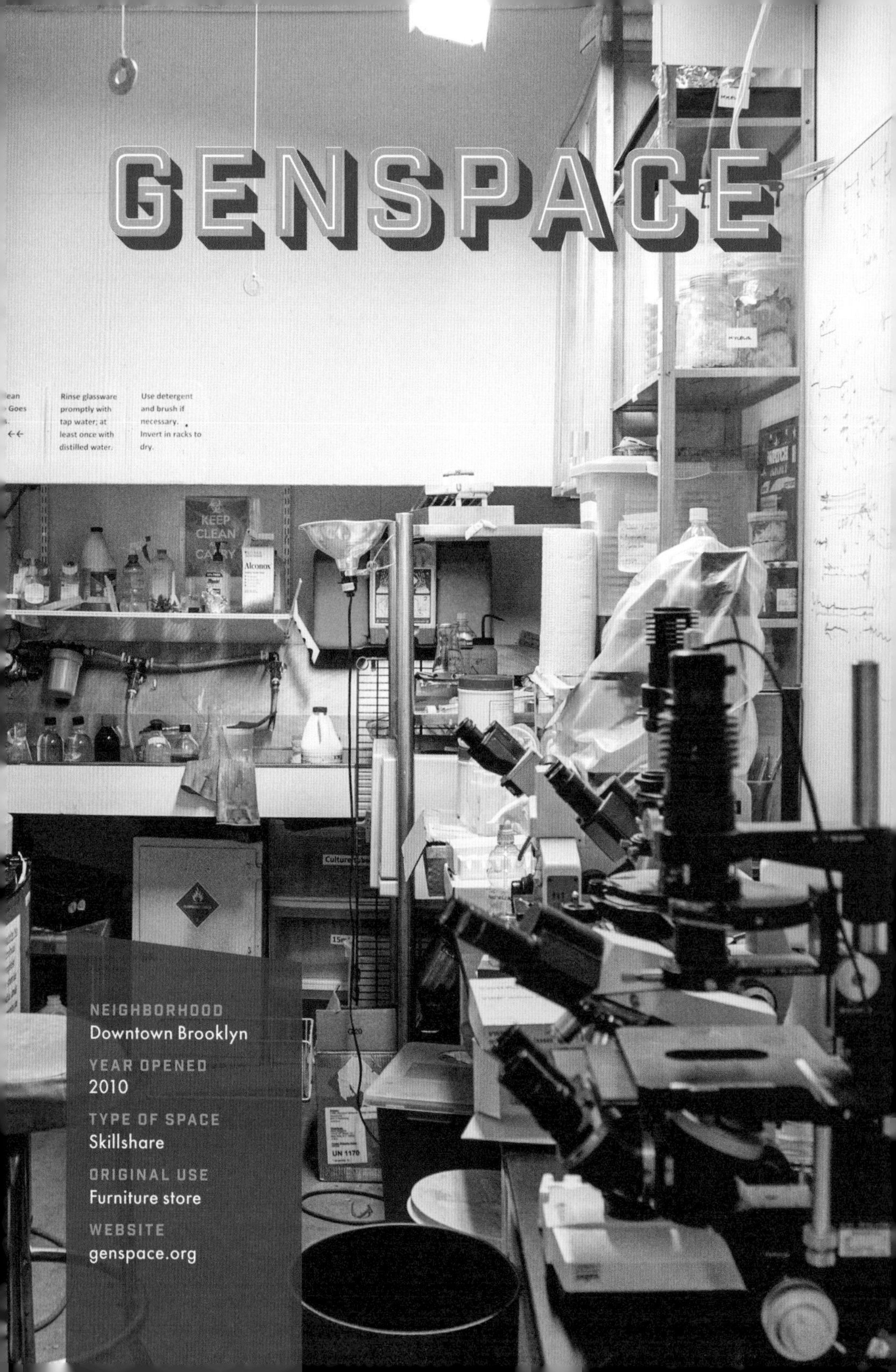

# GENSPACE

Rinse glassware promptly with tap water; at least once with distilled water.

Use detergent and brush if necessary. Invert in racks to dry.

KEEP CLEAN

**NEIGHBORHOOD**
Downtown Brooklyn

**YEAR OPENED**
2010

**TYPE OF SPACE**
Skillshare

**ORIGINAL USE**
Furniture store

**WEBSITE**
genspace.org

**There's a lot more to DIY in Brooklyn than** underground music shows and bike-powered washing machines. Genspace, the first-ever non-profit community biotech lab, aims to demystify scientific processes and give everyone access to the joy of hands-on scientific experimentation. "Members are free to experiment with whatever they want, as long as it follows biosafety guidelines," says molecular biologist Dr. Ellen Jorgensen, Executive Director and cofounder of the space. "It doesn't have to make money; it doesn't even have to make sense. This is a truly innovative space."

Genspace opened in 2010, in a corner of the Metropolitan Exchange building—an unusual space that's quite fitting for a DIY lab. Built in 1917 as the B.G. Latimer & Sons Furniture Company, in the 1930s it became the Corn Exchange Bank, then the Chemical Corn Exchange Bank in the 1950s. In 1970 the building was put on the city's "urban renewal" chopping block, meaning that it could be reclaimed and torn down at any time, and it sat empty until 1978, when it was bought by eccentric designer Al Attara. His dream was to turn the massive

building into a creative startup hive, but since its future was precarious, it languished instead, and Al slowly filled it up with architectural salvage, rescued furniture, cast-off props, and other urban detritus. In 2006 the building was taken off the city's hit list, and since then Al has been slowly cleaning it out and inviting in a wide universe of designers, innovators, nonprofits, artists, and foodies, offering low rent and a collaborative space in which to work. The floors are labyrinthine, with workstations, open spaces, and collective kitchens helter-skelter throughout.

When Genspace came in, Ellen told Al they needed their space to be enclosed but transparent, and possible to decontaminate in accordance with the Centers for Disease Control standards for Biosafety Level 1. So he built them a lab out of old glass doors and metal restaurant counters he had lying around. "Everything he used is repurposed and recycled, which really fits with our ideals," Ellen says. In fact, most of the equipment in the lab was donated, salvaged, or bought secondhand, and Genspace members are working on several open-source lab equipment projects, such as a liquid-handling

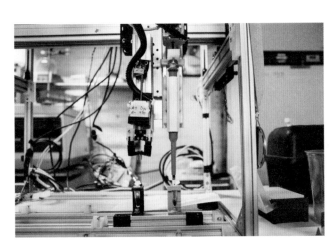

OPPOSITE: Part of the Genspace laboratory, much of which was put together using secondhand equipment. ABOVE: An early prototype of the Opentrons liquid-handling robot, a project spearheaded by Genspace member Will Canine.

robot that can be built for a fraction of the cost of professional models. "I think it's important to show that you can put together a lab on a shoestring," Ellen says. "It's so much more accessible to do modern science than people think."

Genspace attracts a broad spectrum of members, from the curious to the committed. There's a student trying to make super-hardy plants that can survive on other planets, an artist who designs 3D portraits of strangers based on DNA extracted from chewing gum, and a group of scientists engineering *Acetobacter xylinum*, the bacteria found in kombucha. Members are working on an ongoing plant barcoding project using DNA from as far away as interior Alaska and as close to home as Gowanus: in 2014 Genspace partnered with the Gowanus Canal Conservancy to dredge the toxic canal and collect samples in a microbiome survey.

"Doing this has really restored my delight in my own field," Ellen says. "When you see people realize how awesome science is, that's very uplifting." Genspace offers talks, workshops, and classes to engage people who are new to scientific experimentation, ranging from a low-key evening of Polymerase Chain Reaction DNA barcoding over slices of pizza, to Biohacker Boot Camp, an intensive that includes extracting your own DNA, splicing genes, and transforming bacteria. Attendees vary widely in age and background, from students to entrepreneurs to philosophers.

Genspace also engages in a lot of community outreach, striving to bring scientific learning opportunities to underserved communities and citizen scientists from all walks of life. As Ellen said in her TED Talk on biohacking, "If you open up science and allow diverse groups to participate, it can really stimulate innovation."

*Photos by Kit*

Executive Director Dr. Ellen Jorgensen feels that putting a fully functioning molecular biology lab in an unconventional space helps make the technology less alien and invites participation from the community.

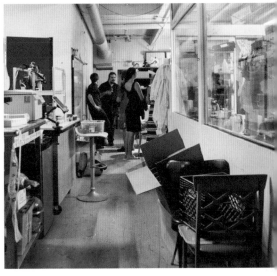

TOP AND BOTTOM LEFT: **PCR & Pizza Night**, a regular open event at the lab for science and discussion, where anyone can come by to learn about DNA barcoding and exchange ideas. BOTTOM RIGHT: The lab, which is compatible with the CDC's Biosafety Level 1 standards, was constructed from salvaged glass doors and metal restaurant counters.

# GOWANUS BALLROOM

**NEIGHBORHOOD**
Gowanus

**YEAR OPENED**
2010

**TYPE OF SPACE**
Art center &
metalworking shop

**ORIGINAL USE**
Cannonball factory

**WEBSITE**
gowanusballroom.com

**"It's a fucking beautiful shithole, this insane** old place," says Josh Young, Gowanus Ballroom proprietor. The cavernous 16,000-square-foot building—formerly a steel mill, before that a chemical plant, and before that a cannonball factory— is now home to Serett Metalworks, a crafting, fabrication, and design firm. Every few months, the space transforms into a venue for massive art and performance spectacles.

Josh came to New York in 1991 when he was sixteen and lived in one of the many derelict East Village squats. Before the turbulent 13th Street Riot in 1995—during which the police, in full riot gear and piloting an armored vehicle, forcibly evicted hundreds of people—Josh helped weld a pickup truck frame to the front door to slow police entry. He's done quite a bit of metalwork for protestors since then, from fabricating metal locking devices in the early 2000s for More Gardens, an activist group protesting Giuliani's eviction of community farms, to working with the Madagascar Institute (p. 126) to build the Illuminator, a van fitted with a rooftop projector, for the Occupy Wall Street movement.

With Serett, the company he started in 1997, Josh channels his creativity into more standard fabrication. Serett has designed and built spiral staircases, shelving and display cases, coal-forged scrolled doors, and metal statues for Ralph Lauren, Woody Allen, Calvin Klein, the Plaza Hotel, and the NYC Parks Department. In 2010 he moved the operation to the Ballroom. "It's either too hot or you can't heat it, and there are always leaks," Josh says. "But look at this place! Everyone who works here loves it."

Everyone who visits loves it too. The semi-regular group exhibitions, curated collaboratively by Josh, Courtney Jordan, Kristin Kunc, George Sferra, and Ethan Spigland, are extremely ambitious, showcasing work from up to fifty artists. The Ballroom focuses on artists whose work would not otherwise find a home and art that engages audiences in unexpected ways. "We strive to unshackle the artist from the art world and its traditional institutions and tastemakers, to dissolve the connection between what will sell and what is shown," George says. "This has helped us support an amazing community of artists, performers, makers, and thinkers."

Past shows have featured huge sculptures, hyperreal paintings, abstract assemblages, quirky dioramas, stained-glass windows, interactive

OPPOSITE: A multimedia group art show entitled "Concerning Matter." ABOVE: The alleyway leading to the Ballroom; a fire-dancer entertaining a crowd during a party.

installations, and shifting projections. Among the many artists whose work has been shown are Swoon, Kiki Smith, Dustin Yellin, Duke Riley, Bruce High Quality Foundation, Tom Otterness, Joanie Lemercie, and Matthew Silver. "This space is great because we do it our way and show what we want," Josh says.

The Ballroom curators are strong supporters of their Gowanus neighbors, as well as emerging and established arts groups across New York, giving space for exhibitions, performances, and fundraisers to groups like Swimming Cities, the Idiotarod, *Nowhere Magazine*, the Brooklyn International Performance Art Festival, Hungry March Band, Arts Gowanus, and the Architectural League of New York. And the support goes both ways: when the Ballroom, which sits on the bank of the Gowanus Canal, was devastated by flooding from Superstorm Sandy in 2012, the

TOP LEFT: Josh Young, founder of the Gowanus Ballroom and Serett Metalworks. TOP RIGHT AND BOTTOM: "Concerning Matter" group art show.

community came out in force to help clean up, raise funds, and put the space back together.

One of the most perfect representations of a Brooklyn underground arts space, the Gowanus Ballroom succeeds beautifully at artistic exhibition, cultural advancement, and creative commerce, all within a gorgeously strange historic building. Josh continues to fabricate bizarre and beautiful spectacles, like a flaming shopping-cart catapult and a pulley system to drop a piano fifty feet onto a tower of champagne glasses. He and the rest of the Ballroom curators are always eager to facilitate art that's bigger, ballsier, and more outrageous. "You got something crazy, something impossible?" Josh asks. "That's beautiful. Call us. Let's make it happen."

*Photos by Alix*

TOP AND BOTTOM LEFT: In 2014, Serett collaborated with the Art Students League of New York on the Model to Monument public art program, through which student sculptures made at the Ballroom were displayed in Riverside and Van Cortland Park. BOTTOM RIGHT: Alexandre Arrecha's "Sherry Netherland," commissioned by the Magnan Metz Gallery.

The cavernous Gowanus Ballroom is one of very few city venues big enough to accommodate large-scale performance extravaganzas, such as HONK! Fest, an annual gathering of activist street bands from around the world. ABOVE: The Hungry March Band.

More from HONK! TOP: Chaotic
Noise Marching Corps. MIDDLE: Environmental Encroachment. BOTTOM:
the massive all-band jam at the
end of the evening.

# HOUSE OF COLLECTION

**NEIGHBORHOOD**
Williamsburg

**YEAR OPENED**
1989

**TYPE OF SPACE**
Artist residence

**ORIGINAL USE**
Bookbinding factory

**WEBSITE**
facebook.com/house.
of.collection

"**The 'collection' in House of Collection is** both a noun and a verb," says Paige Stevenson, a bookkeeper and belly dancer. "We see collecting as a practice, a pastime, and an approach to the world." Nearly every item in this wondrous jumble of a home has been salvaged, found, gifted, or inherited. In the House of Collection, there is as much appreciation and reverence shown to the cluster of rusted garden tools as to the antique Chickering & Sons piano.

The piano was inherited by Paige's partner Ahnika Delirium, a crafter, performer, and Jill-of-all-trades; it was bequeathed by a favorite great-uncle who introduced her to music-making. Many other antique pieces came from Ahnika's family trove, including a cash register from the early 1900s that was used in their Southern Virginia mercantile shop for eighty years. These items live in the conservatory—the room where things are conserved. "The goal is to honor something for what it is, as well as for the value of all the stories that went into it," says Ahnika. Many pieces came from exploring abandoned and derelict places, from Pittsburgh steel mills to Long Island mansions. "I think things become more than the sum of their parts when they're aggregated in this way, in this space," adds Paige.

When Paige moved into the building in 1989, the lower floors were in use as bookbinding and knitting factories, and Williamsburg was a drastically different place. "It was a renegade autonomous zone, full of mind-bogglingly complex and well-produced parties, but also rife with prostitution and crack," she says. Over the years roommates cycled in and out, until Paige was the last one left, and the House of Collection began to take shape. Ahnika moved in in 2007, bringing a complementary aesthetic and philosophy: find beautiful, unusual objects, and display them in a beautiful, unusual way.

There are collections of taxidermy, kitchen utensils, postcards, figurines, Easter eggs, toys, hats, trunks, even plants—Ahnika supposes that they have 111 of those. There's an antique hip-replacement piece, which inspired Paige's original name for the space: The Hip Joint. There are tiny glass bottles pried out of the sands of Dead Horse Bay, earrings Paige made from discarded crack vials she found in the neighborhood, fake greenery from an early-1990s party at the Williamsburg Immersionist warehouse Old Dutch Mustard Factory. There's a box of nails from one of Brooklyn's great lost treasures, the outsider art sculpture Broken Angel House, some of which Paige has used to hang objects around the house.

Yet another thing Paige and Ahnika collect is intensely creative people. In addition to hosting an annual orphan's Thanksgiving with over 60 guests, the couple use their home as a platform to showcase and celebrate the talents of their friends. Their first event was a tasting party for St. Eve's Elixirs, a handmade absinthe potion; since then there have been Burning Man fundraisers, daylong draw-a-thons, a dance and spoken word celebration of Antarctica, burlesque from the Schlep Sisters and Darlinda Just Darlinda, fire spinning, belly dancing, magic rituals, art salons, and sacred circles. Amanda Palmer and Kai Altair have shot music videos, and the Science Channel show *Oddities* filmed a segment there. For the impetuous traveler, a room in the loft is available through AirB&B.

This space may seem like a living museum, but the displays are by no means fixed. "There's a deadening that happens when something is under glass, so we often move things around, because that keeps life in them," Paige says. They both feel that the space is largely at capacity, but it's always tough to say no to a lovely new find. "We know there's a fine line between a curated collection and hoarding," Ahnika acknowledges. "At this point our rule is: don't bring it home if you don't know where it's going to go. But of course we don't always stick to that."

*Photos by Kit and Patricia*

PREVIOUS SPREAD: Paige and Ahnikah in the midst of their collection of collections.

ABOVE: An assortment of lovingly curated displays. LEFT: A box of nails from the Broken Angel House, an outsider-architectural marvel that stood in Clinton Hill from 1979 to 2013. When its creator Arthur Wood was forced to vacate his home in advance of the city knocking it down, he gifted these nails to Paige.

CLOCKWISE FROM TOP LEFT: A few of the House's 111 plants; the "drag buck," dressed in sparkles and feathers by local queer icon Darryl Thorne; a collection of kitchen accessories; the Easter Egg Mobile, assembled from three years of pre-Easter decorating parties, during which blown-out eggs were embellished with all manner of art supplies.

# HOUSE OF YES

**NEIGHBORHOOD**
Ridgewood, East
Williamsburg, Bushwick

**YEAR OPENED**
2007, 2008, 2014

**TYPE OF SPACE**
Performance venue

**ORIGINAL USE**
Brothel, ice factory,
industrial laundromat

**WEBSITE**
houseofyes.org

**Most underground spaces get only one shot,** but the House of Yes—an innovative, ambitious aerial performance venue—has gotten three, weathering serious odds for each incarnation to be bigger and brighter than the last. Over the years, cofounders Anya Sapozhnikova and Kae Burke have gone from self-taught amateur aerialists to some of the most sought-after mainstream nightlife performers in New York City.

In 2006 Anya and Kae, both students at the Fashion Institute of Technology, moved into a huge Bergen Street basement, previously a reggae club, and called it Boring Incorporated. "That was the primordial ooze that became House of Yes," Kae says. They built the space into a series of intricate installations and began transforming it into a gathering space for zealous crafters and burgeoning performers.

That year Anya also founded Lady Circus, an all-female company of acrobats, stilt-walkers, fire-dancers, and contortionists who began performing all over the city, from illegal Brooklyn warehouse raves to swanky Meatpacking District clubs.

Boring Incorporated had its drawbacks, like black mold and flooding. So in 2007 Anya, Kae, and a half-dozen artists moved into what became the first House of Yes, a mazelike space in Ridgewood rumored to have once been a brothel. "That space was intended to be a really collaborative collective, and it was," Anya says. It was also very performance- and party-focused. "At that point we were all really passionate but still very green. Practically all we did was party really hard and try to contribute as much as possible to every event."

OPPOSITE: Cofounder Anya Sapozhnikova and Elena Delgado perform on an aerial apparatus custom built by Flambeaux Fire. ABOVE: Ashley Perez in "The Ambitious Show," co-produced by Lady Circus and the Ambitious Orchestra.

The House of Yes was a deeply loved haven for adventurous artists and revelers, until a toaster fire burned the whole place to the ground in early 2008. The collective lost everything, but the community came through in force to help them get back on their feet: days after the blaze, several prominent underground party promoters, including Rubulad (p. 172), Danger, and Gemini & Scorpio (p. 86), organized a hugely successful benefit at the Financial District strip club Pussycat Lounge. "It made us realize that people really cared about what we were doing," says Anya.

The second House of Yes opened in December 2008, in an East Williamsburg ice warehouse, after three months of DIY renovations. Anya, Kae, and their helpers built out an entire floor, six bedrooms, and a state-of-the-art performance facility with custom-designed aerial rigging. The first full-scale House of Yes production, *The Rusted Gun Saloon*, opened to great press.

"That was a huge turning point for us, being recognized as a performance art circus space, not just a weird underground situation," Anya says. Soon there were high-caliber productions every month, from variety shows to aerial retellings of Spiderman and Peter Pan. For each, the House of Yes family wrote, directed, and produced; they made all the costumes, did all the lighting, built all the sets. "As we got better at things, we were able to produce more, and there wasn't an existential crisis every time of not knowing how to do anything," Anya says.

But after five years of increasingly ambitious shows, in August 2013 the House of Yes received a 50 percent rent increase and lost their home. "It was devastating," Kae says. "I told Anya that I couldn't start over again. But she said, 'Give it six months, you don't know what you're walking away from yet.'" They began looking for a partner to help them make the third incarnation of House of Yes a grown-up, fully

OPPOSITE: A massive Vitamin B dance party. ABOVE: Anya performing in *The Ambitious Show*. LEFT: Anya and Kae in the construction zone of what became the House of Yes 3.0.

TOP: **Flambeaux Fire and Abby Hertz performing in "Shamans & Showgirls."** BOTTOM: **Jen Kovaks in a House of Yes Aerial & Variety Show.**

The staged dance party for House of Yes's 2014 Kickstarter campaign raised an astonishing $92,000—more than 50 percent above its goal—in part due to wild rewards like an octopus massage given by four aerialists, a date with Kae, and, for $10,000, the right to legally change Anya's name.

legitimate venue. "We wanted someone who knew how to run a bar and maybe a restaurant, who had commercial construction experience and believed in the value of what we do. And that's exactly what we got," Anya says. House of Yes 3.0—a 7,000-square-foot performance space, two bars, and a restaurant in a former industrial laundromat—opened in late 2014, a 50/50 collaboration between Anya and Kae, and veteran restaurant industry entrepreneurs Ilon Telmont and Justin Ahiyon.

The new House of Yes is a home for aerial dinner theatre, cabarets, dance parties, film screenings, fashion shows, experimental performances, and any other fascinating thing that comes along. "DIY spaces are a reflection of the people who create them," Anya says. "This is us as artists: we build the shell of these spaces around us, and then we grow." The House of Yes has had an incalculable impact on the rise of Brooklyn's underground, circus, and performance culture, and with partners to handle infrastructure and management, Anya and Kae are able to fully dedicate their passion, innovation, and boundless energy to creative spectacles. Says Anya: "It's not about making a space and that's it; it's about trying to change the world."

*Photos by Maximus and Michael*

# INDUSTRY CITY DISTILLERY

NEIGHBORHOOD
Sunset Park

YEAR OPENED
2011

TYPE OF SPACE
Distillery

ORIGINAL USE
Manufacturing complex

WEBSITE
drinkicd.com

**"We're not like any other craft distillery,"** says cofounder David Kyrejko. "And not in that way of 'everybody's their own special snowflake.' In the way of, like, there's really nothing similar here at all." David and his partner Zac Bruner bring extreme science nerdery and an aggressive DIY mentality to the distilling process, reinventing the entire thing from the ground up. Every aspect of Industry City Distillery's production is done onsite, from growing yeast in a refurbished 1983 bioreactor to distilling in several custom-made machines and printing their bottles' labels on an antique 1935 letterpress.

ICD picked a perfect space for radical making. Bush Terminal, built at the turn of the twentieth century and rechristened Industry City in the 1980s, is one of the oldest and largest continually operating manufacturing complexes in the country. The 6-million-square-foot facility has been home to makers for over a century, and its owners are overhauling the property to upgrade its aging infrastructure and increase its environmental sustainability, with the intention of attracting the next generation of innovators, fabricators, and creators.

The 12,000-square-foot space that houses Industry City Distillery is also home to its parent company, the City Foundry, a research and design workshop that aims to improve small-scale manufacturing. There's a symbiotic relationship between the two: the Foundry provides the tools, space, and intellectual rigor to create new distilling processes and equipment, while the profits from spirit sales help keep the Foundry going.

"We didn't just want to make another vodka, we wanted to make an actually viable urban distillery," David says. "So it had to be small, powerful, energy-efficient, waste-efficient, and yield an incredibly flavorful product." The first problem with that goal? Small, efficient distilling equipment doesn't exist. Early in the exploratory process, David called a company that makes specialized stills with many (though not all) of the characteristics they were looking for, and the quote for a custom system was almost $1 million. So they had to figure out how to make their own.

The result is not one but several pieces of completely unique equipment conceived in the lab by David and designed and fabricated in the shop by Zac, using almost entirely upcycled and rescued materials. "We've developed five different potentially patentable technologies in three years," David says. All the pieces have names: there's IVy—so named because she's the fourth iteration—a continuous stripping still with a separating column that pulls alcohol out of mash more quickly and using less energy than a conventional boiler. There's ßetty (the beta model), a batch-fractional reflux still. "The idea of making vodka using a batch-fractional process is unheard of," David says. "ßetty is the kind of thing you'd see in a laboratory, not in a beverage distillation facility." Most distillers only pull three different cuts from each batch, discarding the first and the last, which have the most impurities. But using a fractional still allows ICD to produce thirty subtly different cuts, which are each tasted and assessed to determine which will be blended into the final product. The result is a far more flavorful vodka that retains a variety of botanical tastes. "We almost didn't call it vodka because it's so different," David says.

ßetty and IVy are prototypes, and they're much smaller than ICD will ultimately need to produce the quantity they're aiming for. Zac is working on completing Victor (the V[th] iteration), which will be able to process 500 liters of mash to ßetty's 57, as well as a new fractioning column nearly three times bigger than the prototype. These pieces will all fit into a tiny alcove, along with the four bioreactors. "We only need 1,200 square feet for a full-fledged production distillery," David says. "We're uniquely situated to go anywhere, which was the idea." So: small, efficient, and yielding a high-quality product. Everything they set out to do.

*Photos by Kit*

TOP: Zac Bruner in the City Foundry workshop, which was constructed to be extremely flexible, making it possible to work with everything from steel to glass. BOTTOM: The City Foundry printshop, with capabilities for silk-screening and letterpress work to make labels and other print products.

CLOCKWISE FROM TOP LEFT: Shop cat Ambassador Scratchy wanders through the City Foundry workshop; ICD's Technical Reserve, the highest-proof spirit distilled in the United States; David Kyrejko breeding yeast; the distillery's tasting room; ICD's custom-designed and -built fermentation system, which fits into a tiny closet; a view of Industry City from the lab.

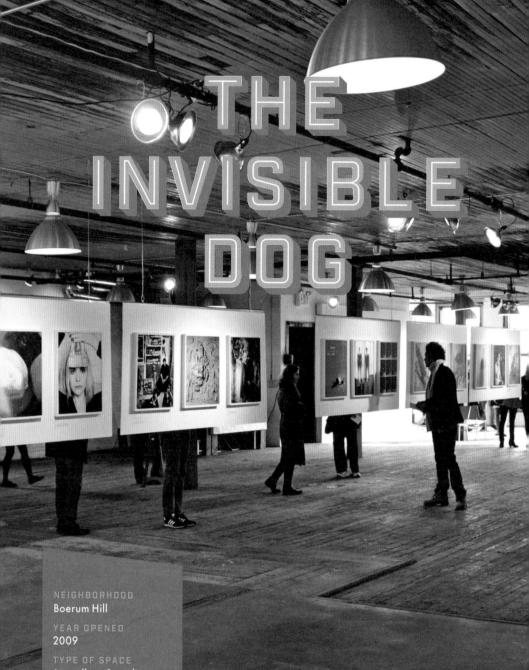

# THE INVISIBLE DOG

NEIGHBORHOOD
Boerum Hill

YEAR OPENED
2009

TYPE OF SPACE
Art gallery & studios

ORIGINAL USE
Garment factory

WEBSITE
theinvisibledog.org

**Named for the novelty toy this repurposed** factory once produced, the Invisible Dog Art Center was started in 2009 by Lucien Zayan, who saw the building while vacationing in New York and fell in love. "I envisioned a multi-disciplinary space with a heart, and the heart is the artists," he says. "And around this heart: exhibitions, dance, music, theatre!" Lucien, who spent decades producing theatre and opera festivals in Paris, had no experience running an art space and had never considered doing so. But he was so inspired that he tracked down the building's owner and improvised a proposal on the spot—"and he was crazy enough to go along with it!"

So Lucien packed up his life and moved to Brooklyn, ready to start realizing his vision. But first he had to clean out the building and make it usable; the three-floor, 30,000-square-foot factory, which was built in the late 1800s, had

over the years produced clothes, belts, beads, and leashes, and it was stuffed with hundreds of years of garments and detritus. So he turned the space into a flea market for three months, which served the dual goals of helping to empty out the space and also letting people in the neighborhood know about the nascent arts center. He sold vintage belts to grown-ups, set up tables full of string and beads for kids to make bracelets, and started talking to artists about using the remaining materials to create beautiful things.

"It's not difficult to meet artists in New York," Lucien says. "Everywhere you go, you have an artist next to you!" Once the second floor was accessible, he built out thirty-five studios and started populating them. Unlike most studio landlords, Lucien vets his artists, and many of the early tenants were inspired by the offer to use the factory's leftover materials. Steven and William Ladd built the gallery's chandelier

OPPOSITE: A solo exhibit of portraits of the "The Artists of The Invisible Dog," by photographer Malcolm Brown. ABOVE: "CATCH" performance series.

out of 10,000 belt buckles, and Ian Trask, the Invisible Dog's first artist-in-residence, created a permanent installation above the doorway using spools of colored elastic.

Lucien's goal is to support emerging artists from all over the world, bringing people from disparate disciplines together to encourage collaboration and inspiration. The Invisible Dog hosts eight visual art exhibits and dozens of events each year, including dance, performance art, theatre, film, and panel discussions. "I love when people come here to see an exhibit and wind up staying for a music performance," he says. "I love when dancers come for a show and see an exhibition on their way in." More than 35,000 visitors come through each year.

In the Invisible Dog's 2012 Kickstarter video, Lucien said, "The presence of the artist, anywhere in the world, in any city, is always a positive addition." He has worked very hard to make the Invisible Dog welcoming to artists and arts appreciators, as well as to an important part of the Boerum Hill community. "Lucien continues to push me," says Ian. "He's definitely propelled me along my artistic journey." Teenagers often come in to show Lucien that they're still wearing the bracelets they made at an Invisible Dog flea market years ago. And he's received great support and praise from his neighbors. "The most important thing is what you give to the artists, to the audience, to the community," he says.

*Photos by Simon*

ABOVE: Chong Gon Byun's art studio. RIGHT: An in-situ installation by Giuseppe Stampone.

CLOCKWISE FROM TOP: R. Justin Stewart's sculptural installation "Distorting (a messiah project, 13C)"; a performance by the Dither Quartet; "It's Later Than You Think" exhibition by Mac Premo; an open-studio visit.

# KNOCKDOWN CENTER

**NEIGHBORHOOD**
Maspeth

**YEAR OPENED**
2009

**TYPE OF SPACE**
Arts center

**ORIGINAL USE**
Glass-making factory

**WEBSITE**
knockdowncenter.com

**Although Knockdown Center is technically** a ways over the Bushwick border into Queens, it feels like a quintessential Brooklyn space: a cavernous old industrial building far off the beaten path that's been repurposed into a multi-dimensional art and event space. Built in 1903 as a glass-making factory, the 50,000-square-foot colossus was purchased in the late 1950s by Samuel Sklar, inventor of a new kind of door-frame called the Knock-Down Door Buck. The Sklars manufactured doors and frames in the factory for three generations, until they moved their production to New Jersey in 2009. David Sklar then took control of the building, with the goal of turning it into a community arts space.

Knockdown Center is in the Maspeth Industrial Business District, surrounded by auto chop shops, bottling plants, concrete manufacturers, and storage facilities. Maspeth is one of the neighborhoods least-served by the NYC subway system, and Knockdown is nearly a mile from the nearest station. But the extra effort it takes to get there is in many ways part of the space's appeal—wandering through a dense industrial streetscape to turn a corner and be suddenly surrounded by light and music and revelry is a particular joy not often available in this chock-a-block, overdeveloped city.

And Knockdown's programming makes great use of the cavernous, versatile space. Events range from family-friendly flea markets to artist-designed mini-golf courses, from underground art parties to huge music festivals. Co-curators and cultural partners include venerable alternative art space Clocktower Gallery, French light artists Nuit Blanche, immersive underground partiers Rubulad (p. 172), and the Queens Council on the Arts. The Red Bull Music Academy has held festivals there two years in a row, and Grammy Award-nominee M.I.A. has graced the stage. Knockdown hosted over 100 unusual cars for the Maspeth World of Wheels exhibition, and partnered with New York art website Hyperallergic to bring London's Lost Lectures series to the United States for the first time, during which thousands of audience members heard talks by transgender model Amanda Lepore, internet superstar Choire Sicha, and porn photographer Barbara Nitke, as well as a performance by Brooklyn urban dance superstars Flex Is Kings. Knockdown has also been used by film and television production companies, with shows from NBC and the Travel Channel filming there.

Michael Merck, Knockdown's creative director, is acutely aware of the space's incredible versatility and the creative opportunities it offers. "Our goal is to present culture in all its forms. We favor projects that respond to our unique architecture and dimensions—but that doesn't necessarily mean that everything has to be big." Per their mission statement, the goal at Knockdown is "to create a radically cross-disciplinary environment that incites surprising collision between otherwise compartmentalized communities." As a result, there's a decentralized programming model, and Michael is eager to engage the community at large. "We find people who are like-minded and are inspired by the space, and we encourage them to use it," Michael says. "It's impossible to find a place of this scale in New York, and I'm so happy to be able to present work in the way it needs to be presented, for as many people as I can."

*Photos by Maximus*

OPPOSITE: Scenes from Red Bull Music Academy's *Hardcore Activity In Progress* festival. OPPOSITE, BOTTOM RIGHT; THIS PAGE, TOP: Bike Cult hand-built bicycle show. THIS PAGE, BOTTOM: Exterior of the gargantuan Knockdown Center.

# THE LIVING GALLERY

NEIGHBORHOOD
Bushwick

YEAR OPENED
2012, 2013

TYPE OF SPACE
Art gallery

ORIGINAL USE
Storefront

WEBSITE
the-living-gallery.com

**The Living Gallery—art gallery, performance** venue, classroom, and community hub—is one of the busiest spaces in Bushwick. Founder and curator Nyssa Frank showcases a broad array of emerging artists, coordinates a wide variety of classes and events, and has initiated several programs to bridge the divide between the neighborhood's incoming artists and its long-standing residents.

Nyssa, a sculptor, singer, and philosopher, has strong art roots: she was raised by artists, and in 2009 she co-founded the Dash Gallery in Tribeca with hip-hop mogul Damon Dash. After that experience, she wanted to open her own gallery, and in 2012 she was offered a great deal on a tiny space in the Loom, a creative retail hub in a renovated Bushwick textile mill. She got a business license and brought a formal proposal to her main investor—her uncle. "People don't like talking about money, but it's a really critical aspect of the art world," says Nyssa. "If people discuss how they were able to start their business,

that can help others understand that they can do it too."

The Living Gallery hosted exhibitions, drawing classes, dance performances, art battles, and more. Within a few months Nyssa had outgrown the space; she wanted more room to do events and the option to curate music shows in a space that didn't close at dinnertime. In early 2013 she moved into a storefront deeper in Bushwick, right on busy Broadway. "One great thing about being here: it's so loud all the time that no one complains about any noise we make," she says. Her landlord, a strong supporter of the arts, also owns nearby bars Lone Wolf and Goodbye Blue Monday, both beloved community hubs and venues for eclectic music and performance events.

"The gallery acts as a platform for curators and artists," Nyssa says, and consequently there are lots and lots of exhibitions. "At first I was like, 'We can only have openings once a month because that's how it's done in Manhattan. But

OPPOSITE: The gallery's backyard is a riot of murals painted by local artists. ABOVE: Living Gallery founder Nyssa Frank performs in CUM BLOOD.

then I remembered, I'm in charge! I can have two a week if I want to." There are exhibits of all types, from "Cósmica," a showcase of Chicana artists from the 1970s, to a solo watercolor show called "Presidents With Boob Faces," to Meryl Meister's hugely popular photo show "Bushwick: Then & Now," which included community performances, lectures, and a historical walking tour. One year for the annual neighborhood-wide art explosion Bushwick Open Studios, the Living Gallery had a BYOArt exhibit, inviting anyone to hang a piece of work on the walls until there was no space left.

Rather than expecting art sales to pay the rent, which would require only showing artists with significant commercial potential, Nyssa keeps the gallery in business by opening her doors

to rentals and a spectrum of events. There are weekly music performances, from jazz to punk to reggae, as well as Drink & Draw classes, potluck performance nights, sonic yoga, career resource sessions, philosophy lectures, the Bookwick reading series, pop-up shops, film screenings, circuit-bending workshops, and the annual Bushwick Fashion Weekend. There's also a slew of kids' programming, from dance classes for tots to Brooklyn Acts for adolescents, spearheaded by a neighborhood mom in early 2013. "This place is a constantly evolving platform for people who need it, whether it's for dance, music, poetry, or community discussion," Nyssa says. "Our goal is to celebrate and enrich this community however we can."

*Photos by Walter*

CLOCKWISE FROM TOP LEFT: A young visitor at the opening of an exhibit by William Tucci; Drink & Draw, a regular figure-drawing evening; art by Dylan J Clarke.

Snapshots of raucous concerts. CLOCKWISE FROM TOP LEFT: The audience at a Filthy Savage show; Vanessa Alvarez of Filthy Savage; Big Neck Police performing at a benefit for *Showpaper*; Adam Aron Amram of Ken South Rock; suichublanco.

# MADAGASCAR
## INSTITUTE

NEIGHBORHOOD
Gowanus

YEAR OPENED
2000

TYPE OF SPACE
Art combine

ORIGINAL USE
House

WEBSITE
madagascarinstitute.com

"When I first started building stuff, I thought, what does the world need? Jet-powered carnival rides," says Chris Hackett, founder and chief fabricator of the Madagascar Institute. Hackett had no background in welding, mechanical engineering, or fabricating, but over the last two decades he and his Madagascar cohorts have brought to life many bizarre and beautiful (and dangerous) creations, like a bike-powered carousel with a flame-thrower in the center and a jet-propulsion swing that powers a blender. Hackett has achieved some notoriety for his ingenuity and vehemently DIY ideology: he has hosted shows on the Science Channel, the Discovery Channel, and TLC, and has been featured in the *New York Times*, *MAKE* magazine, and on VICEtv. Author of *The Big Book of Maker Skills*, he also writes a column for *Popular Science* about surviving the apocalypse in style.

When Hackett started the Madagascar Institute as a machining and performance art "combine" in 1999, he took inspiration from two places:

Survival Research Laboratories in San Francisco, a pioneering group of tinkerers and engineers specializing in large-scale machine performance since the early 1980s, and the Burning Man festivals he attended in the mid-'90s. "Burning Man was violent and cathartic," he says. "It was truly adult entertainment: not that you'd see nipples or hear foul language, but if you didn't watch out for yourself, you might actually die." He wanted to recreate that experience in New York. Madagascar events would be wild, unexpected, and of questionable safety, leaving passersby astounded and bewildered. "I wanted to make dangerous pyrotechnics to go along with spectacle, with wonder," Hackett says.

Of course, he needed to learn how first. He started by hosting "How hard could it be?" drop-in sessions in his Lower East Side apartment, where similarly inquisitive tinkerers would gather to figure out together how a tool worked or an engine was put together. In 2000 he bought a building on the banks of the Gowanus Canal, which gave him enough space to start

OPPOSITE: The delightful chaos of the Madagascar Institute. ABOVE: A MIG/TIG welding class, one of the most popular of the Institute's offerings.

a workshop. What began with a few donated welding machines has grown to encompass two floors filled with just about every kind of tool and material imaginable—scrounged, gifted, dumpstered, and occasionally bought. Once someone in the group becomes proficient with a given machine, the Institute begins offering classes in its use, from welding to etching to 3D printing. "The only thing stopping your idea from becoming real is your own lazy ass," Hackett says. "I want to have everything accessible here: the people, the knowledge, the equipment, the resources."

The Institute is also known for its creative spectacles. There was "Flaming Popes," on the Williamsburg Waterfront, which Hackett describes as "a weird theatrical thing about the schism between the Eastern Orthodox and the Roman Catholics in the eleventh century—with lots of pyrotechnics." There was a guerilla soccer game on Ludlow Street with a flaming ball. "I really like soccer, but you know what the problem with it is? There's nothing on fire." There was a reenactment of the Hindenburg disaster with fifteen-foot dirigibles that burst into flames in Union Square. And then there are the death-defying rides: dueling mechanical bulls, an electrocution seesaw, apocalyptic circus toys, hydraulic mobile sculptures, a 360° swing. Most of the toys are harvested for parts after only a few uses; the joy is in making, not in having.

Madagascar members have made crazy creations at festivals across the globe, from Ireland to Amsterdam to Berlin. At the 2010 Maker Faire in Queens, the Institute put on a build-your-own chariot race that they described as "jankety, cobbled-together, dangerous-to-even-look-at chariots, pedal-powered versus jet-powered versus people pulling a shopping cart, smashing and crashing and racing around a tightly turning track." Entrants ranged from a guy holding a wheel to a giant Kraken powered by a ride-on lawnmower. To complete the spectacle, Madagascar brought flag boys and girls in gold lamé hotpants, a marching band, and trophy ladies covered in body paint. "Everybody just loved it," Hackett says. "You could see the look on people's faces that said, 'I've been waiting for this my whole life.'"

*Photos by Michael and Remi*

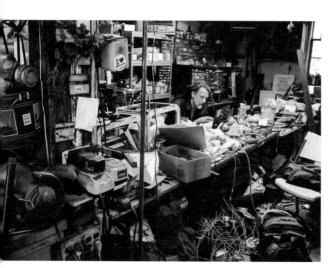 

LEFT: Chris Hackett, master of his domain. RIGHT: The exterior of the Madagascar Institute, embellished with metalwork.

CLOCKWISE FROM TOP LEFT: The Institute's Bridgeport mill; the Jet Fish, a jet-powered carnival ride, built at the Robodock Festival in Amsterdam, 2005; Conrad Carlson and Ryan Johnson setting up JETBIKE!!! at Floyd Bennett Field; a MIG/TIG welding class; Eviction!, a flaming wrecking-ball ride created at Robodock in 2003.

MAS HOUSE

THE COPS
ON O

NEIGHBORHOOD
Bed-Stuy

YEAR OPENED
2009

TYPE OF SPACE
Communal living space

ORIGINAL USE
Laundromat

WEBSITE
n/a

"**We're trying to make this a better city, a** more livable city, and doing it together helps us take care of one another and lessen each person's financial burden," says Rebekah S., one of a dozen anarchist-focused denizens of MAs House, a close-knit community that supports a range of radical ideals like mutual aid, anti-authoritarianism, environmental and social justice, freeganism, and gender and sexual parity. Nearly everything in the house is communal, from food to toiletries to most of the bicycles. Attendance at weekly house meetings—which adhere to nonhierarchical, consensus-based decision making—is strongly encouraged. The dozen-plus housemates, who range from ages 3 to 53, work together on many local and national radical projects, helping one another to engage more fully with their community and the causes they champion.

In the distant past the space operated as a laundromat, but it has been rented out to different clusters of roommates for the last decade. In 2005 it was briefly a DIY venue under the names Snake Dad House and Summercamp; in 2006 a group of rappers moved in and built out a recording studio in the back; in 2008 it changed hands again and became Flushnik, hosting poetry readings and a cyber-theatrical performances. In 2009, anarchist and activist Laurel L. moved in and began putting together the current configuration of the space.

"I had a lot of radical friends looking for a communal living situation, and there was a need for a group home that was politically active and activism-focused," Laurel says. She and friends soon built several new rooms using salvaged materials, and the MAs House community was twelve people strong. "We called it MAs House because whenever people came over we would feed them, like a mom," Laurel says. They also used MA as an acronym that changed regularly, to make the space a bit more difficult to track; some monikers were Mutual Aid House, Mystic Anchovy House, Manarchy Abolishing House,

OPPOSITE: A handmade rack holds all the housemates' rides as well as extra bikes for guests.
ABOVE: All decisions in the house are made by consensus during weekly meetings.

Moldy Apples House, and Militant Anarchist House.

MAs has served as a hub for a wide range of activist projects. All residents were very involved in the Occupy Wall Street movement, Mayday actions, and the People's Climate March. Many environmental justice activists working on Bushwick City Farm (p. 40) and Time's Up (p. 204) have lived there. The housemates champion food justice as well, operating a chapter of Food Not Bombs, a national movement that serves huge meals for free in public parks, made from food reclaimed from restaurants and grocery stores; they have also hosted Grub, a monthly freegan feast started in the early 2000s at Rubulad (p. 172). Another long-running waste-diversion project is the Free Store, through which clothing, electronics, and other goods are donated or rescued from dumpsters and then offered for free to the community. MAs residents have distributed leftist magazines on cargo bikes, conducted anarchist study groups and prisoner letter-writing campaigns, and provided jail support for arrested protestors.

They also host art shows, film screenings, and concerts to raise funds for progressive causes like Earth First, Radical Action for Mountain People's Survival, and the Trans and/or Women's Action Camp.

The house is also, like most communal living situations, a lot of fun. Housemates have face-paint days, zine-reading afternoons, stick-and-poke tattoo nights, and midnight countertop dance parties. They're crafty, whether making practical things like a bicycle-powered washing machine, or silly ones like a birthday piñata in the shape of a pig-faced cop. "We're extremely DIY, although more often it's DIT: do it together," says Emily. Adds Laurel: "You can feed a lot more people with a lot less money, time, and energy if you make one big pot of food together, rather than a bunch of individual meals. It's energizing to support one another and live a positive alternative lifestyle. The whole really is stronger than the sum of its parts, and it's very inspiring to be one of those parts."

*Photos by Kit*

LEFT: Several MAs House roommates, squeezed onto one handmade cargo bike. ABOVE: DIY body shields made out of construction barrels for a Mayday protest.

TOP: A banner made for an anti-capitalist march and displayed outside a Bank of America, which immediately closed for the day when the protestors showed up. INSET: Laurel L., MAs house founder. BOTTOM: A collection of radical political literature and zines made and curated by the housemates.

# MISTER ROGERS

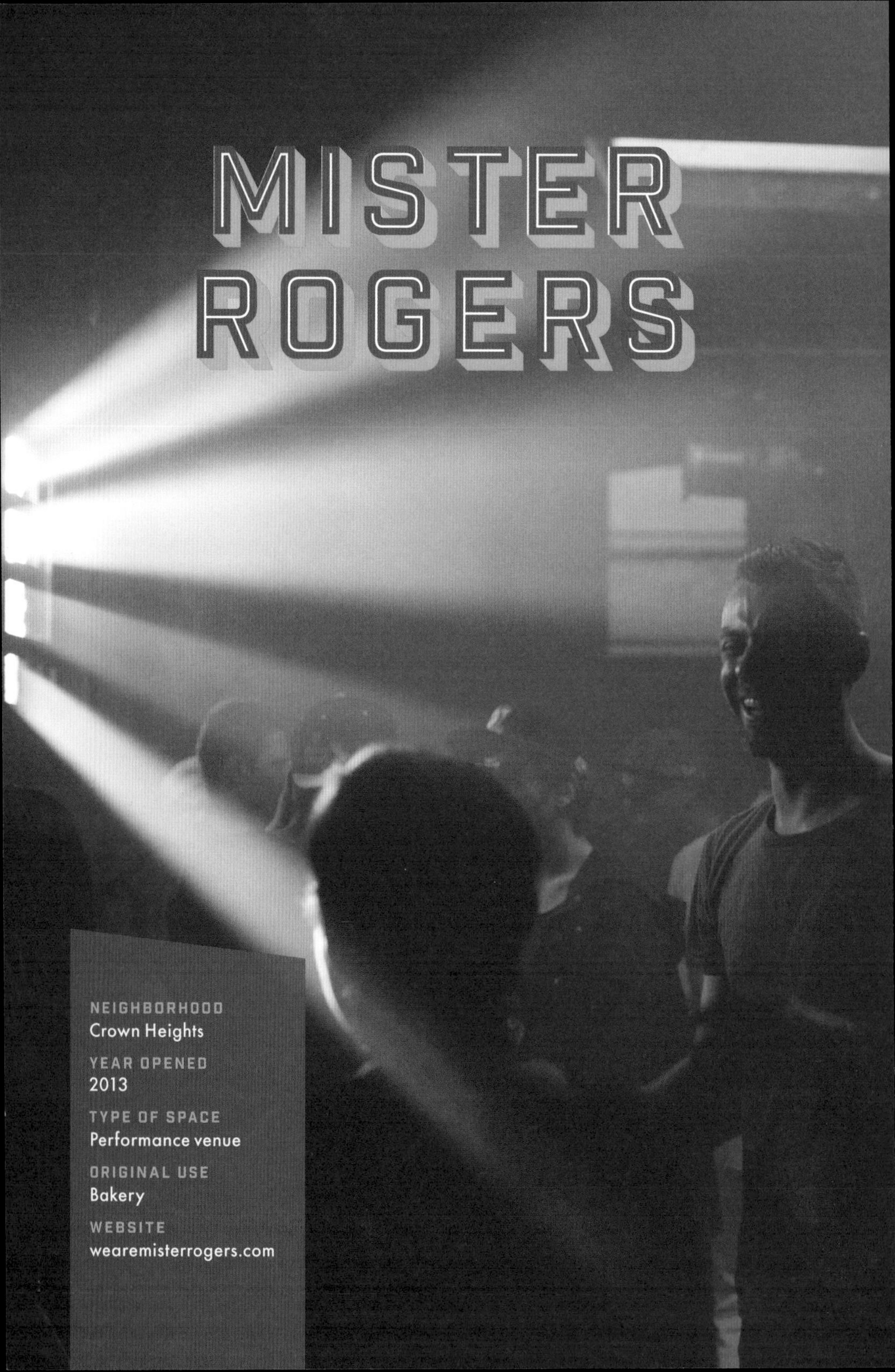

NEIGHBORHOOD
Crown Heights

YEAR OPENED
2013

TYPE OF SPACE
Performance venue

ORIGINAL USE
Bakery

WEBSITE
wearemisterrogers.com

**Mister Rogers, a multimedia event space** in Crown Heights, was started in 2013 by childhood friends Ruvi Leider, Schneur Menaker, and Avi Werde. All three have deep roots in their diverse neighborhood, which has strong Chasidic and West Indian communities, and they're working hard to bring the two very different populations together through a variety of cultural and community events.

Ruvi and Schneur, both photographers, began throwing dance parties on the roof of Ruvi's apartment in 2012. "From the beginning the parties had a great mixture of Jewish kids we knew, plus huge crowds of West Indian people from the neighborhood," says Schneur. "We could see that the lines were really starting to blur." Avi, an events producer, joined the group, and fortuitously the ground-floor storefront became available. What had been Neville Sue's, a West Indian bakery, and then Shark Bites, a Caribbean café, seemed like an ideal place to carve out a much-needed Crown Heights community art space. But first it needed a massive renovation. Neville Sue's had left a twenty-foot-long stove

built right into the concrete floor, stuffed with hundreds of pounds of insulation that took weeks to remove. The trio spent six months ripping down drywall, removing the drop ceilings, pulling up tiles, pouring and painting a new floor, and installing new windows.

The first official Mister Rogers event was a collaboration with the Hoover Dam arts collective, the start of what became a regular series called "For Locals, By Locals," featuring music, comedy, dance, spoken word, and visual art presented by people who live in the neighborhood. Other neighborhood-focused events include the premiere of the documentary *Project 2x1*, exploring the West Indian and Chasidic communities coexisting in Crown Heights, and an exhibition of the "What I Be" project, a touring photography showcase of people with their biggest insecurity written on their faces, which was banned from Yeshiva University. "It has been so gratifying to see different types of people coming together in our space who might otherwise never even talk to each other on the street," says Ruvi.

OPPOSITE: The underground midnight dance party Sublimate. ABOVE: Line down the block for the dance party Balloonacy.

Not all the events are so serious; Mister Rogers has also hosted Balloonacy, featuring 3,000 balloons equipped with LED sensors, and the queer performance party Psychic Spring. And it has become a venue for late-night underground electronic dance parties, inspired in part by the Marcy Hotel, an after-hours dance spot for the EDM set that prominent DJs Wolf + Lamb ran out of their apartment from 2004 to 2014.

During the day Mister Rogers is open for a variety of uses, from yoga classes to bar mitzvahs to film and video production, bringing in increasingly high-level folks, including CNN, Forbes, and Macaulay Culkin. They're planning to add a program called the Mister Rogers Country Club, which would give members access to the space for coworking, rehearsals, and the like.

"We wanted a space we could call our own, into which we could all put our personalities, our love and heart and blood and sweat and tears," says Avi. "And it's been a revelation to see the amount of extraordinary people who walk through these doors, people who believe in culture, in community, in bettering our neighborhood and sticking together." Mister Rogers is a strong addition to a neighborhood undergoing extremely rapid gentrification, providing a venue for creative expression as well as a home for important conversations and community-focused exchange.

*Photos by Ruvi*

CLOCKWISE FROM LEFT: Dance performance during a "For Locals By Locals" event; co-founder Avi Werde serenading the crowd on a small piece of the Desert Forest installation; Trevor Hall performing at the "What I Be" photo exhibition.

TOP: Decorations for the 2014 New Year's party. BOTTOM: CNN setting up studio production for *The Hunt with John Walsh*.

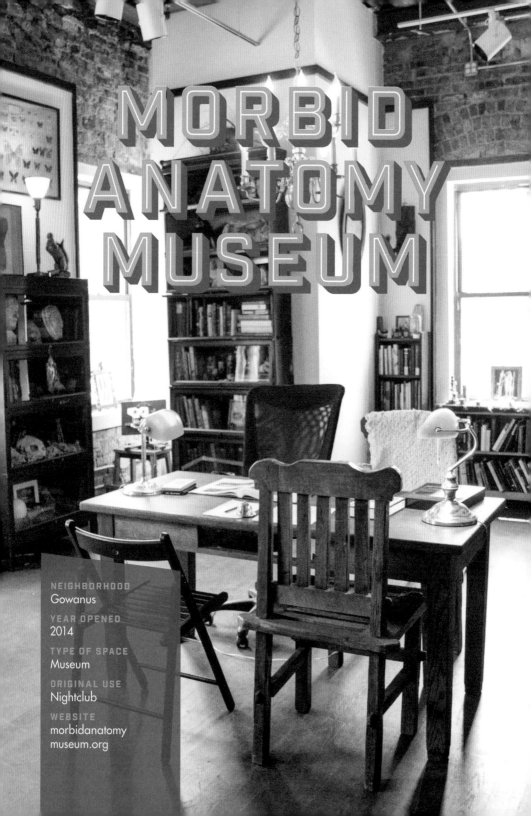

# MORBID ANATOMY MUSEUM

NEIGHBORHOOD
Gowanus

YEAR OPENED
2014

TYPE OF SPACE
Museum

ORIGINAL USE
Nightclub

WEBSITE
morbidanatomy
museum.org

There's probably no other institution in the world that has both a taxidermist and a moulagist on staff, as well as a gift shop featuring creative works by both. At the Morbid Anatomy Museum, a hundred bucks will secure you a "Valentine's Day Syphilis Wax Moulage," a "Two-Headed-Chick Taxidermy Plaque," and many other such curiosities. It's with archaic, creepy arts such as these that the museum strives to combine the beautiful with the strange and to bring to light practices and pursuits that have fallen through the cracks. "We are devoted to forgotten and neglected histories," says founder Joanna Ebenstein. "These are things that don't fit with our idea of the past anymore."

Joanna's tastes have always run dark and slightly strange. "I've always been interested in life—and death," she says. "As a kid, I collected spiders and kept them in my room; I would pick up dead baby birds and my father would put them in formaldehyde for me." Joanna's own collection comprises much of the museum's permanent holdings, from phrenological death masks to antique medical devices. Rotating exhibits have included "Magic and the Paranormal," "Dime Museum Artifacts," and "The Art of Mourning," with the items on display culled mostly from the private collections of like-minded appreciators of the macabre and bizarre.

Morbid Anatomy began as a blog in 2007, after Joanna took a trip to Europe to photograph medical museum artifacts for an exhibition at the University of Alabama at Birmingham. "The blog was my way of sifting through all this crazy material I had amassed, and synthesizing it into bite-size chunks to make sense of it for the exhibition," she says. "It never occurred to me that it would be of interest to anyone else." But it became popular very quickly, drawing together a community of folks who were as interested as Joanna in topics such as Wunderkammers, diableries, memento mori, teratology, and phantasmagoria.

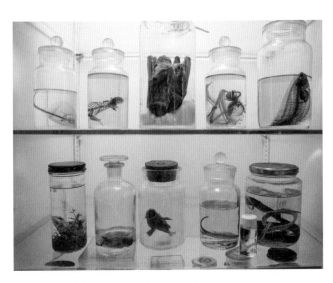

OPPOSITE: The Museum's reading room. ABOVE: Various wet specimens in the museum's permanent display.

In 2008 Joanna became a resident at Proteus Gowanus (p. 158), making her personal book collection, full of gems on the same obscure and macabre topics, available as an open-to-the-public research library. "What Proteus does as an arts incubator is a beautiful thing," she says. "They gave me space, resources, and the tools I needed to figure out what I was doing with Morbid Anatomy."

The community continued to grow, and Joanna began curating an event series with lectures on topics such as the history of skin grafts and the art of spider seduction, an anthropomorphic taxidermy workshop (which was so popular it often had more than 600 people on the waiting list), and even a singles' night—called, of course, Morbid Curiosity. Joanna began lecturing as well, which is how she met twins Tonya Hurley and Tracy Hurley Martin, bestselling YA novelist and producer/brand manager, respectively. When Tracy mused that she'd always thought there should be a museum around this sort of thing, Joanna agreed immediately. "It should happen in this neighborhood and it should happen now," she said without hesitation.

So the three women joined forces to make the museum a reality. In less than a year, a space was procured in a former nightclub, a staff and board of compatriots assembled, and a very successful Kickstarter campaign conducted, netting the nascent institution $76,000 in seed money. The three-floor museum, which opened in summer 2014, has an events space downstairs, a café and gift shop on the main floor, and exhibition galleries upstairs. "I feel like this is my manifesto, what I want Brooklyn to be," Joanna says. "It's a space dedicated to interesting things that doesn't take itself too seriously. If you come here you'll learn something, meet interesting people, and see fascinating things."

*Photos by Alix*

OPPOSITE: Assorted ephemera in the museum's permanent collection. CLOCKWISE FROM TOP LEFT: Part of "The Art of Mourning" exhibition; books in the Morbid Anatomy gift shop; a presentation during the Headless Horseman Variety Show; the exterior of the museum (painted black, of course); an audience gathering before a lecture; a taxidermied two-headed duckling.

# THE MUSE

NEIGHBORHOOD
South Williamsburg

YEAR OPENED
2011

TYPE OF SPACE
Circus training &
performance venue

ORIGINAL USE
Garage

WEBSITE
themusebrooklyn.com

**There's a lot of Williamsburg art history**
in the South 1st Street warehouse—originally
a garage for the Domino Sugar Refinery—that
now houses the Muse. Starting in 2004 it was
Glass House Gallery, a chaotically decorated
"experiential venue" for art, music, and collaborative performance started by Brooke Baxter,
who would go on to cofound the pioneering
DIY music venue Glasslands down the block. In
2010 the space was briefly Live at the Pyramids,
a bare-bones DIY music venue similar to Death
By Audio around the corner (p. 62).

In 2011 dancer and acrobat Angela Buccinni
reinvented the space as the Muse, an aerialist
performance and workshop space dedicated
to fostering experimental creativity in the circus
arts. Angela, a dancer since the age of six and
a graduate of the Boston Conservatory, came
to New York in 2006 to begin her performance
and circus career. Prior to the Muse she ran a
dance studio and performance space in her
Bushwick backyard, but the whole setup was
destroyed by a freak tornado in 2010. After
signing her new lease, Angela reached out to
Williamsburg's circus artists to help build out

the Muse. "Dozens of people popped in once
or twenty times or a million times," she says. "It
was like a social event; we'd cook together and
*then* we'd build. Or I'd melt down and everyone
would hug me and *then* we'd build." In just two
months they had carved out six bedrooms on
two floors, an elevated stage, two bathrooms,
and a kitchen, and put in rigging points throughout the walls and ceilings. Whenever money got
tight, the group would organize a show or throw
a party to raise funds.

The Muse now offers daily classes in a wide
range of circus and performance arts, like
acro-balancing, silks, harness, bungee, trick
ropes, wall running, and juggling. There are
fitness-oriented classes like circus core, flexibil-
ity, hip-hop aerobics, and aerial conditioning.
There are classes for kids as young as five, and
"mommy and me" sessions for babies starting
at eighteen months. In the evenings the space
becomes a performance venue, hosting dance,
acrobatic, and circus performances, as well as
a monthly MuseIAm variety show celebrating
the the vast spectrum of Brooklyn's circus artists.
The space is also rented out for performances

OPPOSITE: Rebecca Collins. ABOVE: The Muse in 2012, shortly after opening, during rehearsals for
*Hot Frosty*, in collaboration with Grounded Aerial.

by troupes that don't have a home of their own, from Grounded Aerial to the Fight or Flight Theater Company.

The Muse operates with an artist-friendly model, whereby choreographers and directors whose shows will be performed there are given rehearsal time at a low cost. "One of the main problems with trying to create art in New York is that it's so hard to survive financially," Angela says. "Artists need time to bask in their process if they're going to create truly profound work, and my fear is that without spaces like the Muse, all our art will eventually have to be imported from other cities that are more supportive."

As with so many small art spaces in Williamsburg, the Muse's future is precarious. Sitting on the border of North and South Williamsburg, it's increasingly surrounded by upscale restaurants and bars, and is a stone's throw from the Domino Sugar Refinery buildings, which will be demolished to make way for a massive complex of luxury condos. As the neighborhood that was once internationally praised as the center of NYC's art and culture becomes more and more hostile toward artistic experimentation, the Muse is at risk of succumbing to careening rents, marking one more casualty of hyper-gentrification and insufficient support of the emerging arts.

*Photos by Maximus*

Performances from the MuseIAm monthly circus and variety show. CLOCKWISE FROM TOP LEFT: Francis Stallings; Frankie Valentine & Sinamon; the Muse's exterior; Kyle Matthew Hamilton.

CLOCKWISE FROM TOP LEFT: **Muse founder Angela Buccinni; an open-floor workout; Tara McManus & Adam H in a fire-eating act.**

# NORTH BROOKLYN BOAT CLUB

NEIGHBORHOOD
Greenpoint

YEAR OPENED
2010

TYPE OF SPACE
Recreation

ORIGINAL USE
Vacant lot

WEBSITE
northbrooklynboat
club.org

**Newtown Creek, which forms part of the** border between Brooklyn and Queens, was designated a Superfund site in 2010. One of the most polluted waterways in the country might seem like a questionable place for a casual paddle, but the North Brooklyn Boat Club, a loose conglomeration of boating enthusiasts, environmental educators, and nautical activists, is working to change that perception. "Going out on the water in New York City is an amazing experience," says founder Dewey Thompson. "Seeing the city literally off the grid, not having any civic apparatus telling you where to go or how to move—that freedom is incredible."

Dewey has been kayaking on the Newtown Creek since the mid-1990s. After the massive rezoning of the Williamsburg and Greenpoint waterfront in 2005, he was concerned that access to the water would become increasingly restricted, so in 2010 he began holding meetings at the Brooklyn Rod & Gun Club (p. 36) to gauge community interest in boating and water activism. "From the very beginning we had an incredibly passionate, participatory, collaborative group," he says. There's Fung Lim,

a boat-builder who has worked with groups like Float the Apple and the East River Apprentice Shop; Jens Rasmussen, an actor, survivalist, and Climate Project Presenter trained by Al Gore; and Willis Elkins, an environmental educator and program manager at the Newtown Creek Alliance—just to name a few. The club's broad focus allows for engagement from people with a variety of interests, from activists to birdwatchers to photographers. "There's definitely a big adventure component too," Dewey says. "Like, 'Is there a way I can risk my life after work today?' There sure is."

The burgeoning club received guidance and support from established boating and environmental groups, as well as several grants. And then came the big coup: Tony Argento, who owns the Greenpoint film production company Broadway Stages, had an unused waterfront lot at the base of the Pulaski Bridge, which he allowed NBBC to use free of charge. Suddenly, the boat club had a boatyard. "Tony has a sort of renegade sense of philanthropy and a deep commitment to the neighborhood," Dewey says. "He liked the idea of people trying to get out on

Resource sharing is a key component of the NBBC mission. Since storing a boat in the city can be quite challenging, members can become Official Paddlers, which allows them access to the club's fleet of kayaks and canoes for personal use.

the water, and was happy for the land to be used in a way that would benefit the community."

Three years later, NBBC is an established nonprofit with nearly 300 members, 30 canoes and kayaks, and dozens of partnerships with community groups, foundations, and local businesses. They've taken more than 1,000 people out onto the water in weekly public paddles and special events like Spooky Halloween Canoe Tours. The boatyard has been outfitted with compost bins, garden plots, a firepit, and several donated shipping containers—two to store the boats and safety equipment, one that holds Fung's workshop for boat-building and paddle-carving, and another to house the Ed Shed, the most visible environmental science aspect of the club, which Willis started in partnership with an environmental-sciences professor at LaGuardia Community College. The goal of the Ed Shed is to facilitate environmental research and education, and its centerpiece is a living Newtown Creek microcosm in a tank, filled with shrimp, oysters, snails,

fish, and even a tiny eel all pulled out of water that many people assume is too toxic to support any life at all. "The creek has a lot of issues, but despite all the damage, there's still an ecosystem, and it's getting stronger," Willis says. "We want to show people that even the most polluted waterways have biological activity."

Club members also participate in citizen science initiatives, including wildlife monitoring, mycoremediation, balloon mapping, and water testing—due to the tidal flow, the water around the boatyard is actually swimmable by EPA standards about half the time. "Canoers and kayakers experience the waterways in a more tangible, hands-on way than anybody else," Dewey says. "We become the eyes and ears on the environmental condition of those waterways, which is a stewardship we take very seriously."

*Photos by Shannon*

OPPOSITE: Getting ready for a public paddle. CLOCKWISE FROM TOP LEFT: Relaxing in the boatyard; paddling on Newtown Creek; a kayaker with her seafaring pup; public paddle heading toward Long Island City; the Newtown Creek microcosm-in-a-tank in the Ed Shed.

# PIONEER WORKS

NEIGHBORHOOD
Red Hook

YEAR OPENED
2010

TYPE OF SPACE
Arts center & studios

ORIGINAL USE
Iron factory

WEBSITE
pioneerworks.org

**Pioneer Works is *huge*. Although not as** big as Knockdown Center (p. 118), at around 27,000 square feet with 40-foot ceilings, it's still absolutely enormous for a city teeming with shoebox apartments and tiny cramped storefronts. It's also, by Brooklyn standards, extremely old, and was neglected for decades. But it's been given new life as a multidisciplinary nonprofit arts hub and learning center, and after a top-down refurbishing, it's a thriving example of creative reuse.

The building was constructed in 1866, burned down and was rebuilt in 1871, and for more than a century was home to Pioneer Iron Works, one of the largest machine manufacturers in the country. The company produced steamrollers and other massive iron machinery, and was so prominent during its heyday that the street the factory sits on was renamed Pioneer Street. After Pioneer Iron Works closed in the mid-twentieth century, the space was used to store paper records for half a century. Then in 2010, prominent Brooklyn artist Dustin Yellin bought the building, planning to turn it into a "utopian art center," with art studios, classes, and large-scale events. But the massive warehouse was just shy of derelict, with no heat, no running water, and minimal electricity. It took about a year of heavy work to get things into shape, including knocking bricks out of more than fifty windows and pouring a new concrete radiant-heating floor.

Less than a year after Pioneer Works opened to the public, Superstorm Sandy decimated the space, which sits about a block from the waterfront. David Sheinkopf, the center's Director of Education, says the whole building was "shoulder-deep in water" after the storm surge receded. It took five months for heat to be restored and classes to start up again. But since then, says David, "we've just grown and grown and grown."

Pioneer Works is getting close to Dustin's utopian dream. The nonprofit has studio space for a dozen artists-in-residence across mediums, a massive exhibition gallery and event space, a slew of classes and workshops, a science lab with a powerful photographic microscope, institutional residencies, a radio show, and a modern art periodical called *Intercourse*.

Classes vary widely, from instruction in emerging technologies like microcontrollers and 3D printing to historical art methods, such as paper marbling and Civil War-era tintype photography. "Demystifying processes is so enabling," David says. "In terms of computing, the open-source movement put greater power and knowledge in the hands of the individual. By applying that model to education, we're helping to open what has become essentially a locked system." The programming also includes semester-length classes that offer a platform for rigorous learning without the constraints of traditional hierarchies. The goal is "to give artists greater access to new processes, a new vocabulary, and equipment and instruction that would otherwise only be available in a private institution," says David.

Pioneer Works's events are similarly eclectic. On a given evening, there might be a lecture on fly genetics or faking your own death, a selection of locally made short films, or musical performances by acts ranging from Spiritualized to Slavic Soul Party to Omar Souleyman.

The arts center is a strong cultural addition to Red Hook, and works closely with neighboring organizations such as the Red Hook Initiative and Dance Theatre Etcetera. "There's such a strong community here, and a real neighborhood feel," says David. "It's like nothing I've experienced anywhere else in New York."

*Photos by Maximus*

Pioneer Works hosts a monthly Second Sunday art and performance event, featuring open studios, lectures, site-specific "art interventions," and live music curated by Olivier Conan, founder of the Park Slope music club Barbès.

TOP AND BOTTOM: Musicians inside the space and revelers outside during a summer Second Sunday. INSET: Dustin Yellin's 2013 piece *400 BC*, a mixed-media collage made of hundreds of pieces of paper suspended in layers of translucent glass.

# POWERHOUSE ARENA

**NEIGHBORHOOD**
Dumbo

**YEAR OPENED**
2006

**TYPE OF SPACE**
Bookstore & event space

**ORIGINAL USE**
Cardboard factory

**WEBSITE**
powerhousearena.com

**Daniel Power has been taking big risks in** the publishing world for twenty-five years. In 1995 he started powerHouse Books in his East Village apartment; his goal was to "publish artistic output, primarily photography, that expressed compelling visions and perspectives, particularly those on subcultures, photojournalism, or unusual personal projects." The conventional wisdom at the time was for a publisher to aesthetically unify all its books, so it was clear they all belonged under the same umbrella. "I was very much against that," says Daniel. "I wanted each book to be radically different—in size, page count, design—like they weren't related at all except for the logo on the spine."

powerHouse has remained true to those early ideals, continuing to release a vast and varied list of groundbreaking and critically acclaimed works. "It's a very large house of wildly varying subject matter, in content and in form," Daniel says, "hence the capital H in the name." Some triumphs include *Women Before 10 A.M.* by Véronique Vial, their first bestseller in 1998; four acclaimed books by Helen Levitt, an NYC street-life photographer whose work spans seven decades; a series of monographs from Jamel Shabazz, photo-chronicler of hip-hop in the late

1970s; and *New York September 11*, created in partnership with Magnum Photographers. That book was shot, designed, produced, and brought to market in less than two months, and has sold 300,000 copies, enabling power-House to donate over half a million dollars to the 9/11 Neediest Foundation. "After September 11th everyone wanted to go and dig," Daniel recalls, "but Mayor Giuliani kept saying, 'Just do what you do best; that's what will bring New York back.' Well, we make books. We wanted to create something visceral; we wanted the pure emotion of what the tragedy was like for so many that day."

In 2006, powerHouse moved into the stunning 10,000-square-foot Dumbo arena, in one of the rebar-enforced concrete behemoths where industrial engineer Robert Gair invented and manufactured corrugated cardboard at the turn of the twentieth century. The building's previous tenant had been the avant-garde theatre company GAle GAtes et al., known for their large-scale immersive shows, which had been one of the first arts organizations in Dumbo when they arrived in 1997. Dumbo was still somewhat sleepy when powerHouse came in. "When we moved here you'd see about five people a day

The repurposed arena was designed by award-winning architect David Howell and includes arena seating, 175 feet of windows, exhibition galleries, and, of course, endless stacks and shelves of books.

walking over the Brooklyn Bridge," Daniel says. "Now it's like a parade, this giant flowing river of humanity."

It took seven months to build out the Arena, molding it into a light-filled, industrial-chic combination of publishing company, carefully curated bookstore, gallery, and event space. The Arena's first event was the 2006 VH1 Hip-Hop Honors Awards, which brought in more than 2,000 people, proving immediately that the company could handle serious crowds. The Arena has hosted massively popular book launches, including new work from Joyce Carol Oates, Paul Auster, Al Gore, Anthony Bourdain, ?uestlove, and Jonathan Franzen, as well as Brandon Stanton's bestselling *Humans of New York* and David Sedaris' *Let's Explore Diabetes with Owls,* which lasted nearly eight hours— "Sedaris talks to every single person," says Daniel, "and he will *not* be rushed."

In non-book events, powerHouse often holds art exhibitions as part of the annual Dumbo Arts Festival; they hosted the launch of Spike Lee's Absolut Brooklyn vodka, the Creators Project, Brooklyn urban dance troupe Flex Is Kings, and a seemingly endless list of cultural luminaries. "We just want to keep doing things that spark the imagination," Daniel says.

*Photos by Remi*

CLOCKWISE FROM TOP LEFT: A group art show in the powerHouse gallery; a book launch party; powerHouse founder Daniel Power; the bookshop registers.

The staircase is a comfortable place to lounge and provides extra space for the audience during events.

# PROTEUS GOWANUS

NEIGHBORHOOD
Gowanus

YEAR OPENED
2005

TYPE OF SPACE
Art gallery & arts center

ORIGINAL USE
Box factory

WEBSITE
proteusgowanus.org

**"One of the most challenging things about** Proteus Gowanus is explaining it to people," says Co-creative Director Tammy Pittman. Her partner and the space's founder, Sasha Chavchavadze, agrees: "Describing it succinctly hasn't really been done." So what goes on in this nonprofit interdisciplinary arts center, housed in a 1900s box factory on the banks of the Gowanus Canal? A lovely jumble of semi-related artistic and creative projects, each of which in some way connects art, artifacts, and books.

"Proteus Gowanus is very much a reflection of this space," says Sasha. "The building itself is a sort of artifact." The entrance is in the back, down a narrow alley. "I think there's something exciting about the setup," Tammy says, "feeling as though you're walking into a sort of alternate universe, or a secret." The centerpiece of the space is an exhibition gallery and reading room where curated collections revolve around yearlong exhibition themes, many of which are inspired by the neighborhood. "I think going deep into the place you're in is a good way to ground a community," Sasha says. "And Gowanus is such a wonderful, culturally rich place." Along with each year's visual art exhibition are a slew of thematically linked events, from workshops to symposia to performances.

Radiating outward from the main gallery are several other projects, many of which grew out of past exhibits. "We tend to view the projects-in-residence as having incubated here," Sasha says. "We've helped them survive by giving them reasonable rent and sharing resources." Among these is the Reanimation Library, a collection of odd and out-of-print books that "lack privileged cultural status and/or market value." There's also the Fixers Collective and the Writhing Society, groups that meet regularly for "improvisational fixing and mending" and to "practice the techniques of constrained writing," respectively. There's the Observatory

OPPOSITE: "Hall of the Gowanus" permanent collection, which includes marvels like nineteenth-century *Brooklyn Eagle* clippings about the canal, as well as the official Superfund Site Sediment Sample, gifted by the Environmental Protection Agency in 2011. ABOVE: The Reanimation Library, a curated collection of out-of-print relics, chosen primarily for the images they contain.

event series, presenting lectures and discussions exploring "the realms where art and science, history and curiosity, magic and nature overlap." There's Morbid Anatomy, which began as a private collection of books and cabinets of curiosities and has grown into its own museum (p. 138). And there's the Hall of the Gowanus, a community-curated micro-museum of artifacts, maps, documents, and many other bits and bobs having to do with the canal on whose banks Proteus Gowanus resides. The thread connecting all these disparate projects seems to be a passion for interdisciplinary creating, as well as a longing to form a community around personal passions or obsessions, whether that's Oulipo, anthropomorphic taxidermy, or just finding ways to make broken things run again.

"I hadn't planned to do all this, it just sort of happened," says Sasha, who has had an art studio on the premises since the early 1990s. When the building was put on the market in 2005, she and nineteen other artists came together to purchase it. Tammy, who has a background in public health but has always made art on the side, came by in 2007 to help Sasha with an exhibit, and she never left.

When Sasha started the project, she was feeling disconnected from the art world. "The whole process of being an artist and communicating your work seemed really deadly and competitive," she says. "It felt antithetical to what art should be, which to me is very organic and essential and life-enhancing." She hoped Proteus Gowanus would unite a community of artists and thinkers, and it has; in the process it has also restored Sasha's joy in her own artistic practice. "This space has enriched my life by inventing a new environment in which I can function as an artist."

*Photos by Remi*

Named for the Greek sea god who could change his form, Proteus Gowanus is a constantly shifting organism, growing and changing to encompass new and different creative pursuits.

CLOCKWISE FROM TOP: A launch party for a book produced by Proteus Gowanus' publishing arm, Proteotypes; co–creative directors Tammy and Sasha; an art opening in bkbx, a gallery and exhibition space inside Proteus Gowanus.

# RED LOTUS ROOM

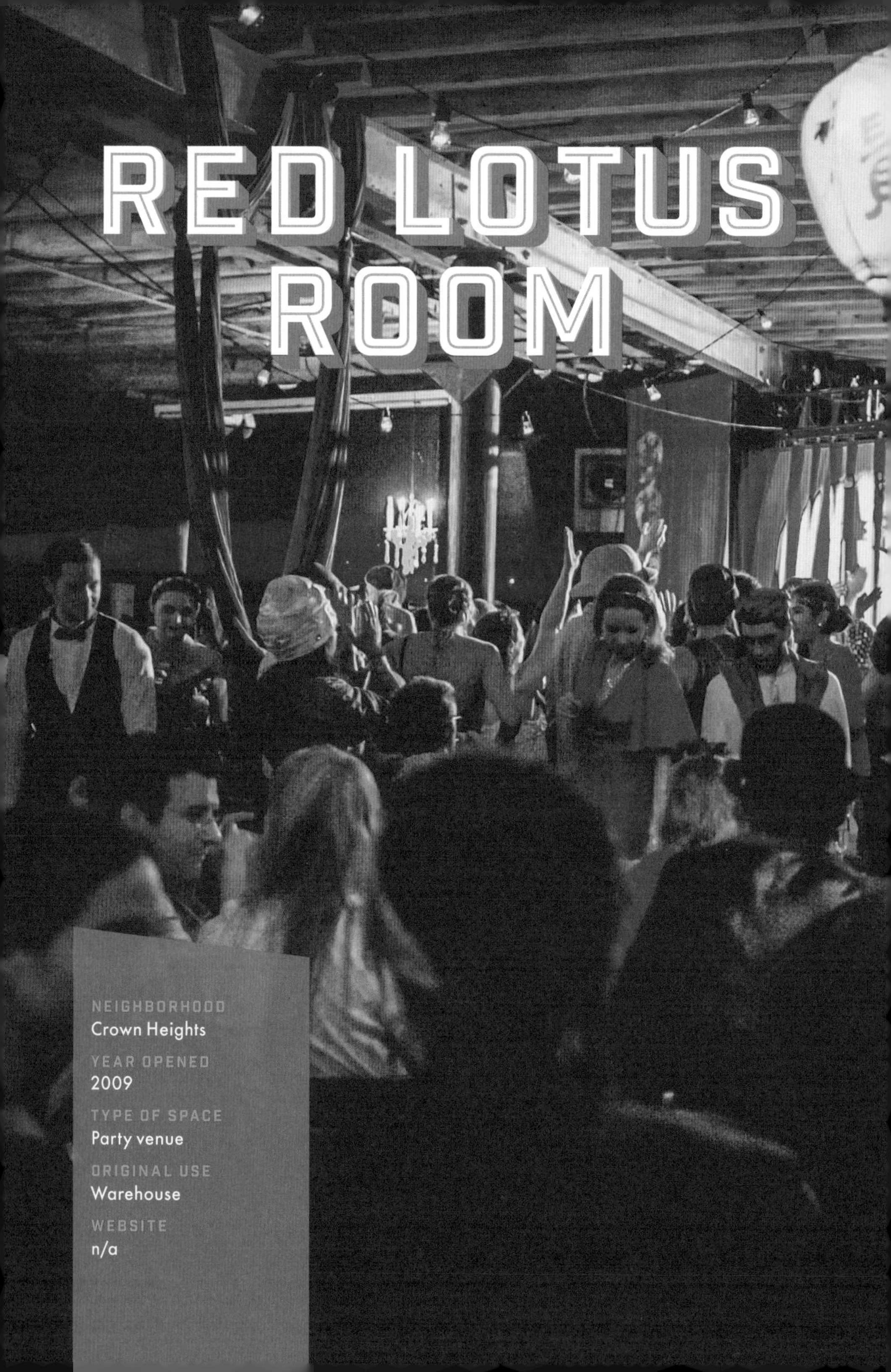

**NEIGHBORHOOD**
Crown Heights

**YEAR OPENED**
2009

**TYPE OF SPACE**
Party venue

**ORIGINAL USE**
Warehouse

**WEBSITE**
n/a

"I just don't think there's enough glamour in the world," says Juliette Campbell, proprietress of the Red Lotus Room, who has worked very hard—and very successfully—to bring a healthy dose of glamour to Brooklyn's nightlife. Juliette, who came to New York in the 1980s at eighteen to become a Broadway actress, watched New York change drastically over the years, becoming increasingly hostile to underground culture. In response, she decided to open a speakeasy. "I wanted it to feel like a 1920s nightclub in Paris or Berlin or Shanghai, which all had very decadent underground scenes," she says. In 2007 she threw her first themed party, called Shanghai Mermaid, in a Dumbo basement. Guests in period attire walked down a desolate street, through an unmarked door—"and when they stepped inside it was just complete glamour. I wanted people to feel like they'd been completely transported."

The party was a hit, so Juliette threw another and another. She took Shanghai Mermaid to several different venues while searching for a permanent home, which she found in 2009: a beautifully decrepit 6,000-square-foot Crown Heights warehouse, which had been left empty for more than twenty years. Soon the walls were draped with red velvet, lanterns were hung all about, and guests swarmed in, decked in a riot of feathers, ruffles, sequins, and fringe. Shanghai Mermaid quickly became one of the most immersive parties in Brooklyn.

Each soirée had a different theme: Dragon Ball, Weimar Cabaret, Bastille Day, Old Hollywood. The parties went past dawn, with elaborately costumed revelers watching a dazzling array of performers and dancing to period-music. A cross-section of Brooklyn's talent graced the Red Lotus Room stage, including burlesque dancers Veronica Varlow and Amber Ray, fire-spinners Reina Terror and Flambeaux, aerialists Seanna

OPPOSITE: The best-known Red Lotus Room event was the (nearly) monthly Shanghai Mermaid party, for which guests were required to dress to a different evocative theme each time, and bands and performers entertained late into the night. ABOVE: Drew Nugent and the Midnight Society.

Sharpe and Anya Sapozhnikova, and bands Blue Vipers of Brooklyn, Baby Soda, and Hot Sardines. Shanghai Mermaid helped launch the careers of many of these artists, especially the "hot jazz" bands.

The Red Lotus Room inspired not just revelers and performers, but other party producers as well. Six BANZAI!!! extravaganzas took place there—huge exhibitions curated by nightlife impresarios Eric Schmalenberger and Muffinhead, displaying the work of visual and installation artists alongside drag acts and DJ sets. Dr. Sketchy's Anti-Art School, the Hoover Dam collective, *CoilHouse* magazine, and queer activist group Quorum Forum all threw fêtes. Burning Man camps had fundraisers and activist groups had benefits; there was erotic art, body painting, an all-male circus, and a queer disco. In 2012 Hollywood came to call, when the Coen Brothers filmed scenes from *Inside Llewyn Davis* there.

And then it all ended. In 2013 the building was sold to a developer, and it will likely be demolished or turned into condos. It's a great loss, and speaks to the lightning-fast gentrification of Crown Heights: the sale price for the building was over $1 million, more than six times what it sold for in 2006. "Brooklyn is just a dollar sign for the developers and the city now," Juliette says. "They don't care about community or art, or that performance and creative nightlife is a big part of what makes New York magical."

Juliette has gone back to a nomadic Shanghai Mermaid, although the next Red Lotus Room is in the works. "The parties are a tremendous amount of work, but it's so rewarding to do this and to share it with wonderful people," she says. "Whenever I walk through a party, people grab my arm and say, 'Thank you so much for doing this.' That means a lot to me."

*Photos by Erica and Michael*

Seanna Sharpe performs aerial with Arishka Kil, her pet python.

CLOCKWISE FROM TOP: **Zazoo in wild finery during a Blunderland party; Iggy Berlin sings with accordion accompaniment by Patrick Harison; Anya Saphhznikova performs at Shanghai Mermaid.**

CLOCKWISE FROM TOP: Drew Nugent and the Midnight Society at Shanghai Mermaid; Christine Geiger at Shanghai Mermaid; The Pixie Harlots backstage at a Blunderland party.

CLOCKWISE FROM TOP: Stormy Leather at BANZAI!!!; founder Juliette Campbell in the dressing room; Eric Schmalenberger and Muffinhead at BANZAI!!!; Juliette introducing performers; Darrell Thorne at Shanghai Mermaid.

# ROYAL PALMS

DO NOT WALK ON COURTS

**NEIGHBORHOOD**
Gowanus

**YEAR OPENED**
2013

**TYPE OF SPACE**
Recreation

**ORIGINAL USE**
Die-cutting factory

**WEBSITE**
royalpalmsshuffle.com

During a trip to Florida in 2010, Jonathan Schnapp and Ashley Albert decided on a lark to visit the world's largest shuffleboard club, Mirror Lake, in St. Petersburg. Both Jonathan and Ashley had fond memories of playing the game with their grandparents as children, but they were astonished at the party they found in Mirror Lake: there were live bands, veggie hot dogs, a bookmobile, and a huge crowd of twenty- and thirty-somethings having a blast. "I took one look and thought, 'People in Brooklyn would freak out over this,'" Ashley says.

Neither Ashley or Jonathan have a background in anything shuffleboard-related. They each boast a varied, Brooklynish résumé: Ashley is a voiceover actress, lead singer of an indie kids band, and jewelry designer; Jonathan is a web developer, professor, DJ, and piñata-maker. But when they came home from Florida, they started casually looking at real estate, "mostly to convince ourselves it was a really bad idea," Ashley says. A shuffleboard court is 6' x 60", so the likelihood of finding a space large enough to accommodate many lanes, as well as being affordable and accessible, seemed extremely unlikely. But a few months later they walked into a former die-cutting factory on the Gowanus canal, and they knew they had to do it. "The building didn't look like much, but we were able to see the possibilities," says Jonathan. "The location was really perfect, and so was the column spacing—it would enable us to fit in the courts."

"We just plunked down our life savings and started figuring out how to make this happen," Ashley says. They worked on it for two years, and were able to have a soft opening at the end of 2013—the 100-year anniversary of shuffleboard in America. They spent a long time raising money: "All of our investors are individuals," Ashley says, "a lot of first-time investors, a lot of local people, and a lot of women, which I'm really proud of." They also did a Kickstarter campaign for the actual courts, which raised over $40,000—more than twice its goal. "That gave us a lot of confidence," says Jonathan. "It showed us how many people were excited to support this idea and help it grow, to make our passion project their passion project."

As Ashley and Jonathan hoped, the somewhat archaic game, long relegated to retirement homes and cruise ships, is doing swimmingly in Brooklyn. It's the perfect intersection of nostalgia, novelty, and challenge—"shuffleboard takes a minute to learn but a lifetime to master," Ashley says. "It's hard to be very, very good, but it's also hard to be very, very bad." Plus it's a very social game. "It's flirty, like, 'Hey, we're going to knock each other out,'" says Jonathan. "And of course, you can play it with a drink in your hand."

The community aspect of the club is readily apparent. One Kickstarter reward granting membership into the Monday night shuffleboard league was so popular that a Tuesday night league was added as well. And shuffleboard experts around the country have taken happy notice of Royal Palms. "It's a very small, tight-knit community, and they welcomed us so warmly," Ashley says. "They're thrilled that the game they love might get another life, that a new generation might play it."

*Photos by Alix*

TOP: The bar, which serves homemade ginger syrup and other drink accompaniments. BOTTOM: A few of the 10 courts. "We knew we wanted a shuffleboard club with a bar, not a bar that had one shuffleboard court in it," says cofounder Ashley Albert.

"Even though this is a big glossy place, it's really a mom-and-pop organization," says Ashley (bottom, with cofounder Jonathan Schnapp).

# RUBULAD

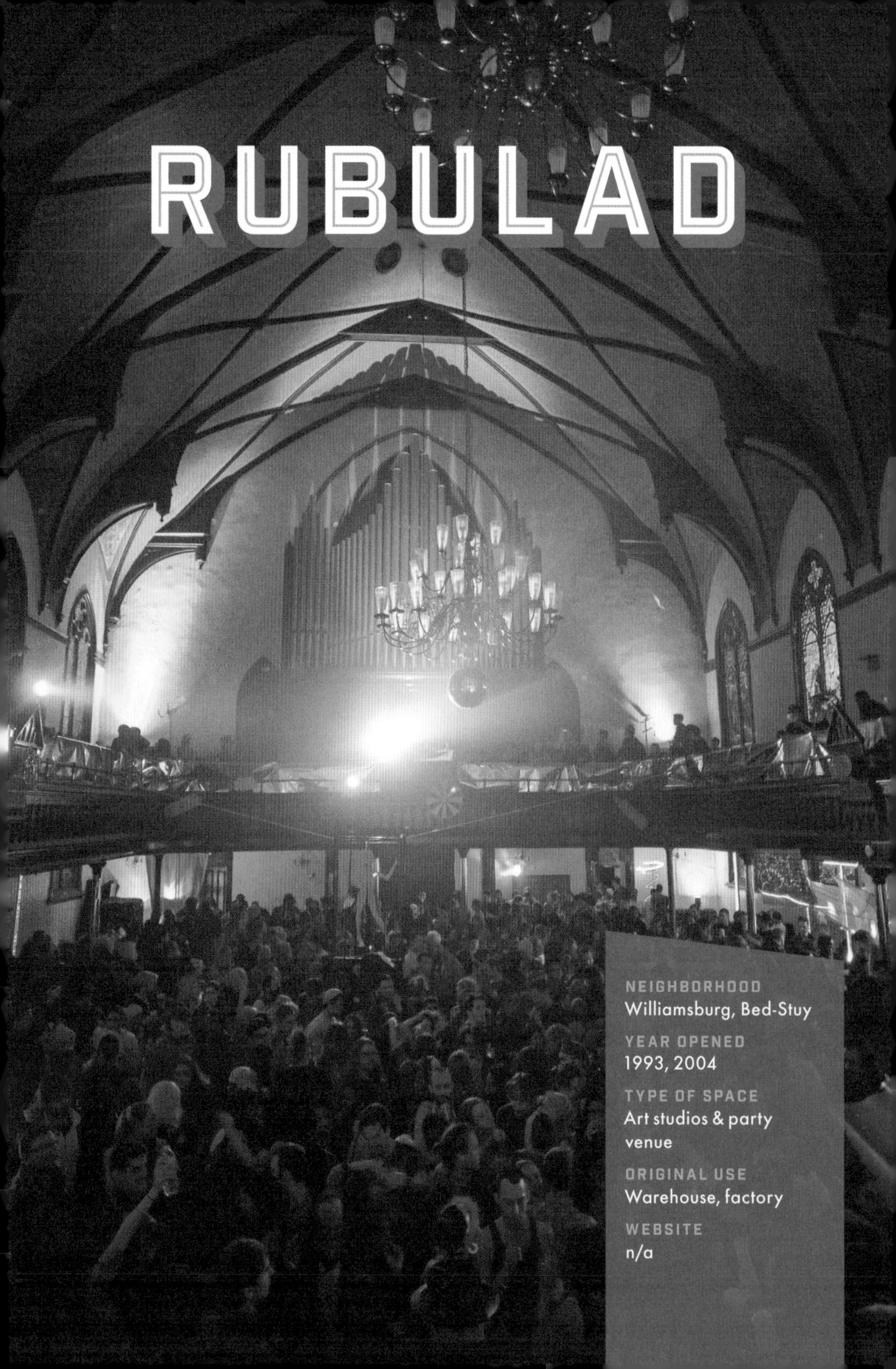

NEIGHBORHOOD
Williamsburg, Bed-Stuy

YEAR OPENED
1993, 2004

TYPE OF SPACE
Art studios & party
venue

ORIGINAL USE
Warehouse, factory

WEBSITE
n/a

**The matron saint of Brooklyn's creative** class, Rubulad is the longest-running underground art party in the borough. Since 1993, founders Sari Rubenstein and Chris Thomas have been staging wild rumpuses with huge casts of collaborators, in two different homes and through many nomadic years. In a city that seems more and more determined to repress underground nightlife and cultural experimentation, Rubulad continues to create secret playlands to celebrate immersive art and unbridled creativity.

Sari, Chris, and several other musicians moved into a warehouse under the Williamsburg Bridge in 1993—the same building where the art collective Lalalandia had run El Sensorium, a restaurant/"aquatic experience" where food was served on tables covered in moss, drinks were handed through curtains of water, and light and video projections made it look like all surfaces were made of liquid. Lalalandia were the champions of the late-1990s Williamsburg cultural movement Immersionism, and Rubulad embraced the same sensorial overload. "My dream was to create a holistic piece of art, a collaborative, experiential environment that many people had a hand in," Sari says.

The first Rubulad event was a carnival-themed extravaganza, with art rides, games, performers, and music throughout the space. Everyone who lived there, and an ever-widening family of creative collaborators, participated in planning, crafting, and performing. Soon to be a more-or-less monthly affair, each Rubulad party had a theme—Night of the Living Toys, Paradise Fruit Stand, Laundry Day, Mysteries of the Deep, Disco of the Damned—and guests were encouraged to dress accordingly. In a labyrinth of rooms, there would be a DJ here, a performance artist there, a nook filled with colored pillows, giant puppets on the roof. There were plenty of what Sari calls "indescribable acts" as well—someone dancing in a dress made of flaming hula-hoops, a theremin-and-singing-saw serenade, looping antique Scopitones. "Rubulad has been the seed bed where so many people have been able to grow and flourish," Sari says.

In 2002 Rubulad was priced out of their Williamsburg home. After being itinerant for a

Though the Rubulad crew lost their space in 2011, they haven't been sitting idle; instead, they've thrown wild parties in a slew of surprising locations, from a derelict Bushwick church to a Greenpoint production studio. OPPOSITE AND ABOVE: Party Monster's Ball, Rubulad's 2012 April Fools party.

couple of years, in 2004 Sari and Chris moved into a 1920s factory at the edge of Bed-Stuy, previously the home of another underground event space, and before that an after-hours gay disco. They hosted Rubulad there for nearly a decade, with half a dozen artists living and creating upstairs, and the parties downstairs getting crazier and more beautiful. "We aim for it to be like, you can't even decide which room to be in because they're all so wonderful," says Sari. Remnants from each fête were incorporated into the space's décor: the walls, ceilings, rooftop, furniture, backyard, and garden teemed with a dizzying array of decorations, from framed shellacked jellybeans to glitter-coated stuffed animals to an enormous birdcage with a carousel horse inside. Rubulad also hosted a slew of smaller and more intimate events, like Grub, a monthly feast made from food diverted from the waste stream—i.e., donated or dumpstered.

Then in 2011, the Department of Buildings served Rubulad with a vacate order, in a sudden crackdown that included several other semi-legal art spaces. Sari & Co. took the show on the road once again, creating their fêtes wherever they could, from a sound stage in Long Island City to an abandoned church in Bushwick to the Knockdown Center (p. 118). Despite raising $35,000 on Kickstarter, Sari and Chris have been unable to find another home for Rubulad. "We're not actually a business, and it's hard to explain to a potential landlord that we've been doing something for twenty years but have no paperwork to prove it," Sari says.

Rubulad has always drawn a strong, diverse community of the adventurous and the curious. "One of the things I really treasure is that it's such a mixed audience," says Sari. "When you see a Chasidic guy talking to a Radical Faery, that's really magical." And so the search to carve out a safe space for collaboration, experimentation, and underground culture-making continues. "I'm trying to be optimistic, to believe that we can do it again," Sari says.

*Photos by Alix, Julia, and Tod*

Rubulad fosters a culture of collaboration in everything that goes on, from making art to playing music to eating dinner. OPPOSITE AND ABOVE: Grub, a monthly feast of dumpstered and donated food for friends and co-conspirators—"sort of like a soup kitchen for artists," says founder Sari Rubenstein (opposite, top right).

OPPOSITE: **Rubulad's Brasstastic Blowout, part of the 2014 HONK! Fest.** ABOVE: Props, décor, and accessories from more than a decade of parties adorned every inch of Rubulad's Bed-Stuy space. "We really tried to never un-decorate anything; we just put more stuff on top," says Sari.

# THE SCHOOLHOUSE

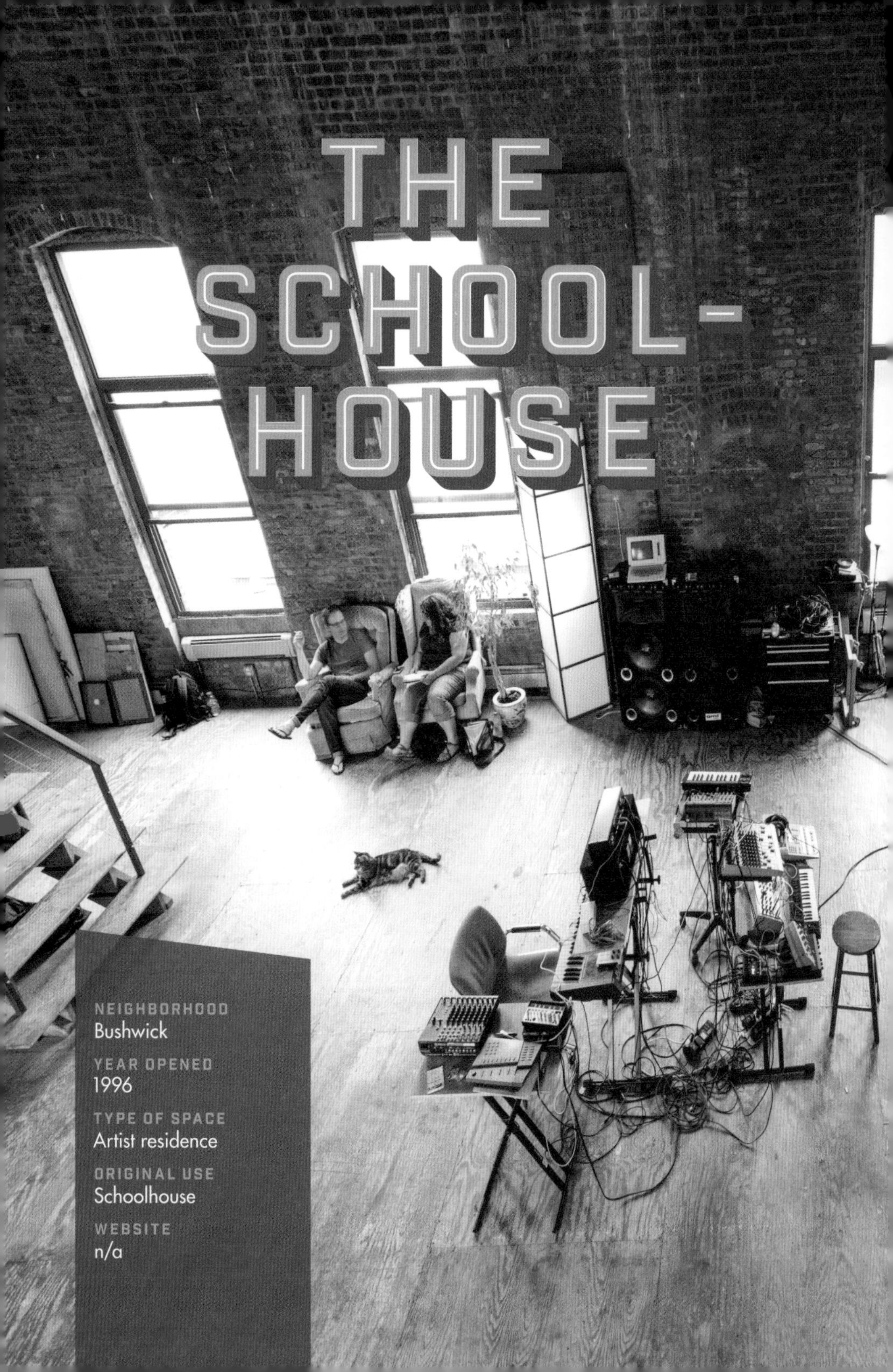

**NEIGHBORHOOD**
Bushwick

**YEAR OPENED**
1996

**TYPE OF SPACE**
Artist residence

**ORIGINAL USE**
Schoolhouse

**WEBSITE**
n/a

**"I've never seen anything like it,"** says musician Willy Muse. "You walk into this place and just feel creative energy all around you." With more than twenty artists, musicians, and filmmakers living and creating in a huge old school building, it would be hard not to.

Brooklyn Public School 52 was built in 1883 and served as an arts-intensive elementary school until 1945, when it was sold—for $27,050 cash—to a manufacturing company to be converted into a factory. Fast-forward fifty years to 1996, when a twenty-something artist named Erin McGonigle found it listed as a rental in the *Village Voice*. Recently the victim of a massive fire, the building was derelict and strewn with debris; it took Erin and some friends half a year to get it into livable shape. They viewed the project as a social experiment and called themselves ORT—"organizing resources together"—to convey the collaborative lifestyle they championed. In 2000 they opened the second floor, bringing in five more roommates.

By 2001 the third floor was livable too, and eight more people came onboard.

Mark Dwinell, frontman of the cosmic synth band Forma, coordinates the third floor and has been living in the Schoolhouse since 2003. He estimates that more than fifty roommates have cycled through, running the gamut of creative pursuits, including visual arts, music, design, jewelry making, screen-printing, and mobile art. Many have gone on to excel in their fields: Yale drama critic Sunder Ganglani, dancer and the Smithsonian's chief of visitor experience Samir Bitar, fashion photographer David Linton, composer Keiko Uenishi, poet Ariana Reines, costume designer Kaibrina Sky Buck, and Grace Exhibition Space founder Jill McDermid have all lived in the Schoolhouse. "I love the space and the type of energy it attracts," says photographer Mariette Papic. "No matter where I go, it pulls me back and inspires me to work."

Built in 1883, the Bushwick schoolhouse was designed in a modified Italianate style by James W. Naughton, the Superintendent of Buildings for Brooklyn's Board of Education. The roll-down gate now features a mural collaboration by street artists Nychos, Sheryo, and The Yok, painted in 2013.

The Schoolhouse denizens often open up their unique space to the community. "A big thing about this place is having people bounce ideas off each other, inspiring one another to be greater and to dream bigger," says musician Dave Powers. Over the years, the group has held block parties, curated salons and visual art shows, and hosted magazine launch parties for *Supermachine*, *Table Talk*, and *Kingbrown*, the latter featuring live mural painting by street artists Nychos, The Yok, and Sheryo. There have been myriad music shows as well, including Neutral Milk Hotel frontman Jeff Mangum, Blues Control, Black Dice, Wolf Eyes, and international experimental artists like French guitarist Richard Pinhas and Steve Hauschildt of Emeralds.

Mark feels it's his duty to preserve the noble old building. "Fighting against decay in a place like this, it's a lot of work," he says. But as a musician, he has always appreciated the unique acoustical and visual opportunities the space offers. For over a decade he's been curating semi-regular shows, generally electronic or experimental music, as semi-private affairs. "I really love having events," he says. "I don't run a bar; I'm not interested in this as a money-making venture. But putting on a good show, letting people experience this amazing place—that's a real pleasure."

*Photos by Maximus*

Despite decades of mistreatment and abandonment, the Schoolhouse retains many architectural details from its distant past. Bedrooms, studios, workshops, and kitchens make innovative use of the strangely shaped rooms and cubbies, turning the imposing building into a warm, art-filled home.

# SECRET PROJECT ROBOT

NEIGHBORHOOD
Williamsburg, Bushwick

YEAR OPENED
1998, 2011

TYPE OF SPACE
Art studios & music venue

ORIGINAL USE
Warehouse, auto-body
repair shop

WEBSITE
secretprojectrobot.org

**Secret Project Robot is part of the old** guard of North Brooklyn art spaces. It began in Williamsburg as Mighty Robot, started by multimedia artist Eric Zajaceskowski in 1998; six years later, Eric, Rachel Nelson, and some friends renamed themselves Secret Project Robot and took over one floor of the underground art and music complex Monster Island, in the warehouse that had been the original home to Flux Factory (p. 74). The collective spent seven years there presenting vivid, immersive group art shows and performances from up-and-coming Brooklyn bands, including Cult of Youth, Knyfe Hyts, Dum Dum Girls, and the Yeah Yeah Yeahs, who, despite a Grammy nomination, chose to have their tenth-anniversary show at the 150-capacity space in 2010.

At the end of 2011 Monster Island lost their lease, and Secret Project Robot moved into their current space: a former auto-body repair shop in Bushwick. The space is still run by Eric and Rachel, who were married in Secret Project Robot's backyard. Though no longer a collective per se, many of the original members are still involved. "We collect certain people," says Rachel. "People who make sense here find us and stick around forever."

In its current incarnation, Secret Project Robot is a nonprofit hybrid music and art space featuring a gallery, two stages, and twenty-seven artists spread across eight studios, including three soundproofed repurposed metal freight containers. The studios are inexpensive for the neighborhood: "We want the cost to reflect the spirit of what we're about," says Rachel, "which is supporting artists and creating a healthy environment for people to work and create together." The visual artists share a maximalist aesthetic,

OPPOSITE, ABOVE, AND NEXT PAGE: Scenes from Bushwig 2014, an annual alternative drag festival, which featured more than 160 performers over two days and nights.

with an emphasis on color and installation. "Making art part of your daily life, making it surround you, getting lost in making something for hours—art should be like a kid's playground, usable, accessible, and fun," Rachel says.

Secret Project still brings in well-known bands like Spiritualized, Black Dice, Quintron, A Place to Bury Strangers, and Oneida, who have been involved with the group from the start. The space also presents a vast array of performances, from Bushwig drag spectaculars to the Ende Tymes experimental noise fest, and immersive art shows like "You Are Here," a life-sized maze filled with sculptures and time-based art events.

Rachel, who has a master's degree in political science and economics, never expected to find herself running an art space. "I'm interested in development theory and post-Marxist economic thought, so I guess this is a social experiment. But I love it! It's such a nice way to live."

The space's rent in Bushwick is triple what the Monster Island space cost in the 2000s, and in 2013 Rachel and Eric opened a low(er)-key bar a few blocks away called Happyfun Hideaway, which helps fund Secret Project. But despite the price tag, everyone is thrilled with the location. "There's such a strong ethos in Bushwick right now," says Rachel. "The people who come here have a determination I've never seen anywhere else." Secret Project Robot has a strong relationship with their neighbors and the community, and they view Bushwick's explosive gentrification with dismay. "Artists are not the gentrifiers," Rachel stresses. "There's a moment when co-existence is really possible and everyone works in unison to make a better community, and it's not art that destroys that. It's the people who want to come and leech off of creativity."

*Photos by Maximus*

ABOVE: Secret Project friends Quintron and Miss Pussycat entertain a yardful of revelers at the Spring Fever Festival, 2013.

# SILENT BARN

**NEIGHBORHOOD**
Ridgewood, Bushwick

**YEAR OPENED**
2004, 2013

**TYPE OF SPACE**
Living space, art galleries,
music venue

**ORIGINAL USE**
Textile factory, house

**WEBSITE**
silentbarn.org

**"People are always trying to define DIY,"** says Katie McVeay, Silent Barn's Press Chef. "Ten years on, the Barn is still 'doing it ourselves,' but this time around we're doing it a little differently." Silent Barn is in fact pioneering a radical new take on DIY: intentional, transparent, and fully legal, not to mention consistently innovative. The massive collective is making it up as they go along—to great success.

Silent Barn was an early entrant into Brooklyn's wild DIY music scene: it started in Ridgewood, Queens, in 2004, when the band Skeletons began putting on all-ages shows in the kitchen of the repurposed textile factory they lived in. The musical offerings were always inexpensive and extremely varied, from hardcore to hip-hop to chiptune, and the space was popular and well-loved. But in July 2011, the Department of Buildings ordered the residents of the Barn to vacate because they were illegally living in an industrial space. Mere days later, the building was ransacked and about $15,000 worth of equipment was destroyed or stolen.

That could have been the end, but instead the collective launched a successful Kickstarter campaign, raising $40,000 toward a new space. "We got so much support from the community, so it was our responsibility to do things the right way," Katie says. "We decided to focus on longevity." This meant finding a new space that was legally zoned for both living and hosting performances. (The Ridgewood space eventually became a new music venue called Trans-Pecos; see p. 208.) It took nearly two years for the collective to find a mixed-use space that was big enough for its growing community, but in early 2013, Silent Barn 2.0 opened its doors in Bushwick.

The new incarnation is a continuation of the first Barn on a much bigger scale. The building itself is larger—three floors, eight bedrooms, twelve art studios, thirteen roommates, three stages, two galleries, and a huge yard. In addition to an eclectic range of music nearly every night, the Barn has been host to science art, multimedia video events, a monthly "adventurous dinner club," theatre groups in residence, a barber shop, the Aftermath Supplies artist reuse center, the nonprofit Center for Strategic Art & Agriculture, a rooftop garden, and a recording studio in a trailer. "Silent Barn acts as an artistically inclined autonomous zone, where we get to make the rules and share the work we want and are excited by," says Joe Ahearn, who has lived and worked in both Barns.

"Silent Barn is giving vitality and substance to the concept of constructing our own world," says collective member Nathan Cearley. The space's organizational structure is completely non-hierarchical, volunteer-run, and consensus-based, with about 150 people participating. Administration is framed on the metaphor of a kitchen: there are about 60 Chefs, each responsible for a small aspect of the Barn, from booking shows to buying toilet paper. "We have weekly Kitchen meetings with all the Chefs, and part of that is Stew, which is all of our discussion topics, whether it's what murals are coming up or how to deal with conflict resolution," Katie says. "Everything goes in the Stew and we work it out together."

The Barn isn't only focused internally. As Kunal Gupta, who has lived at both Barns, puts it: "The thing that matters is the promise of this strange experiment producing something of value to the world, via a successful community-building pathway to our direct neighbors, and thereby to the city as a whole." Barn members regularly attend community board meetings and do outreach in the neighborhood, and they have worked with senior centers and afterschool programs. "We're finding any way we can to be a positive force, because we're going to be here a long time," says Brandon Zwagerman, the Outreach Chef.

The parameters and goals of the Silent Barn are constantly shifting and expanding. Arielle Avenia, who runs Aftermath Supplies, says, "I love navigating this whole-made-up-of-parts and all the interesting drama that brings about, while ultimately having a community of people who've got each others' backs." Eli Lehrhoff, the Art Chef, agrees: "We've managed to corral so many brilliant people here, and force their conflicts and concordances into creating something truly new and exciting."

*Photos by Alix and Walter*

Some energetic Silent Barn acts. PREVIOUS SPREAD: Ken Minami of Ken South Rock. ABOVE, CLOCKWISE FROM TOP RIGHT: eskimeaux; Terror Pigeon; Shady Hawkins; Japanther.

ABOVE, CLOCKWISE FROM TOP LEFT: Hieroglyph Thesaurus; Mannequin Pussy; Amour Obscur; Warper block party.

TOP: The installation "Dear Childhood I Have Dreamed of You" by Chrissy Reilly. BOTTOM: Deep Cuts record store and barbershop.

CLOCKWISE FROM TOP: Silent Barn's resident theater company Title:Point performing *Salish*; the DIY indie videogame-making collective Babycastles began in the original Silent Barn and maintains a presence at this one; art installation in a Silent Barn hallway.

# SPECTRUM

**NEIGHBORHOOD**
East Williamsburg

**YEAR OPENED**
2011

**TYPE OF SPACE**
Rehearsal space, party
venue

**ORIGINAL USE**
After-hours bar

**WEBSITE**
facebook.com/The
SpectrumBK

**The Spectrum opened in late 2011, right** around the time that the House of Whimsy, transgender artist Mx. Justin Vivian Bond's East Village loft and gathering space, was being demolished to make room for condos. Several other queer community and collective living spaces had also recently been evicted in Bushwick, Flatbush, Park Slope, and beyond. Performance artists Gage of the Boone and Nicholas Gorham—who had been Mx. Bond's roommate—were looking for a new space for queer and queer-friendly artists to gather and present their work.

They found what would become the Spectrum tucked behind a cheap diner in East Williamsburg. A former aerobics studio and after-hours bar, the space was painted black, walled with mirrors, and adorned with a stripper pole and two disco balls. "It was grimy and sleazy," Gage says, "but also so weird and beautiful." Furnishing the space happened organically, and mostly for free. Couches came from friends who ran a vintage furniture store, mannequins appeared after a performance event, some big decorative pieces were sent over by a friend working on a fashion shoot. "The way the space came together, it's like the Spectrum has a mind of her own," Gage says. "She says, 'I want *those* chairs. I want *that* as my bar.' We've got to give her what she wants; she's very high maintenance."

Gage has spent time in squats in Barcelona, warehouses in Copenhagen, and a collective in San Francisco, and he's taken inspiration for the Spectrum from all of these: "They're social hubs, places where there's a lot of support for people living alternative lifestyles, trying to focus on art and music and drag, making that sustainable." The Spectrum is plugged into this international community, and artists from across the world stop by to visit, perform, or just pitch in. "At any given moment someone might appear out of the blue and say, 'I can help! But I'll only be in town for three days,'" Gage says.

During the day, the space is used for rehearsals—dance, performance, theatre, or anything else. The hourly rate is low, and can even be paid for in trade: an hour of rehearsal for an hour of

Artists performing at *Revolting Grace & Execution,* a monthly dance and performance series. OPPOSITE: **Monstah Black.** ABOVE: **Mel Elberg.**

work on the space. Many evenings there are classes, like disco yoga, queer pilates, self-defense, dance, and meditation. All are offered on a sliding scale, and all have a focus on inclusivity for any identity or body type. "We want people who are trans or female-bodied or queer to feel like this is a safe space," says Gage. "It's an open door for them to walk through."

Then there are the nighttime events, which showcase art and performance of all kinds. Some recurring shows include Cloud Soundz (a music showcase), Revolting Grace and Execution (performance and dance-based work), Dicktionary (poetry reading), Mama Said Sparkle! (performance art), Intercourses (interview-style discussions with queer pioneers), and Ova the Rainbow and Dizzyland (elaborately themed late-night dance parties). Community feedback about the space has been extremely positive, and three years in, Gage feels the Spectrum has really hit its stride. Nicholas has left to focus on his own creative pursuits, and Gage now runs the space with help from a collection of volunteers. "I feel like this is my radical duty, my everyday activism," he says. "It's a labor of love, and it comes from a radical lineage and lifestyle."

*Photos by Kit and Shannon*

TOP: Dance performance. BOTTOM: Gage of the Boone. OPPOSITE: A Queer Yoga class.

# SUPERHERO
# SUPPLY CO

NEIGHBORHOOD
Park Slope

YEAR OPENED
2004

TYPE OF SPACE
Nonprofit tutoring
center

ORIGINAL USE
Candy store

WEBSITE
superherosupplies.com

In 2002, bestselling author Dave Eggers and award-winning educator Nínive Calegari opened a pirate-themed store at 826 Valencia Street in San Francisco. The shop is a cute bit of subterfuge: although it stocks eye patches, scurvy-be-gone pills, and siren-song silencers, it's really a front for a nonprofit student tutoring and writing center. The model has been a great success: 826 Valencia serves more than 6,000 students per year, and seven other 826 incarnations have been launched across the country.

The second of these, opened in 2004, is the Brooklyn Superhero Supply Company. The Park Slope storefront was the site of several retail establishments over the years, from a candy store to an appliance outlet. The goods on offer now are far more interesting: an array of capes and secret identities, bottles of truth serum, jugs of invisibility, and cans of omnipotence. New products are added often by store manager Chris Molnar, who is always working to come up with "new things a superhero would obviously need."

Tucked behind the shop, the 826 tutoring center offers a "third space" for students, distinct from home and school. About 2,500 kids come through each year for afterschool tutoring, class field trips, and writing-based workshops. Says Executive Director Joshua Mandelbaum, "We provide the students, most of whom come from families where English is not the primary language, a chance not just to strengthen their skills, but to think about writing in a much larger way, as a means of self-expression."

Every 826 program is imbued with the same sense of exuberant creativity with which the Superhero Supply Co. was conceived: there's a STEM writing workshop about the zombie apocalypse, a personal-statement weekend for high-schoolers, and a workshop about "marketing as storytelling" in partnership with the branding agency CBX, which teaches students how to become 826 brand ambassadors from behind a lemonade stand. "We want students to see what they can do with the things we teach them," says Joshua. "The CBX workshop is one example of showing students that there are people who make a profession out of using these skills." There's also an annual Summer

All 826 centers follow the same model: a nonprofit tutoring program in back and a quirky street-facing retail shop in front. Other shops include the Greater Boston Bigfoot Research Institute, Time Travel Mart in Los Angeles, and Robot Supply & Repair in Michigan.

Filmmakers Intensive in which students write, direct, and film a ten-minute short film in two weeks. The films are then professionally edited and screened at the Brooklyn Academy of Music.

There are around 250 active volunteers involved: manning the shop, running workshops, leading field trips, and tutoring drop-in students. "Volunteers are very much the engine that runs this place," says Joshua. Also helpful are the clever fundraisers that support the 826 mission, from Scrabble for Cheaters, where participants raise money to invent new words, to the BBSCo Spring Collection, where fashion designers like Opening Ceremony and Jack Spade create capes and other crime-fighting apparel for auction. "We love events we can use our unconventional support system to foster," Chris says.

The programming all works in harmony, and the center is very successful, with waitlists for all the workshops and more in-schools requests than the group can serve. And everyone involved with the space is extremely proud to be part of it. "As someone on the administrative fundraising end of a nonprofit," Joshua says, "being in this amazing space with all these super hyped-up students doing incredible work is just so rewarding."

*Photos by Alix*

The Superhero Supply Co offers crucial crime-fighting merchandise and tools, including mental enhancements like bravery and telekinesis, body add-ons like telescopic armature and ocular zoom implants, and a Capery for proper outfitting.

# THE SWAMP

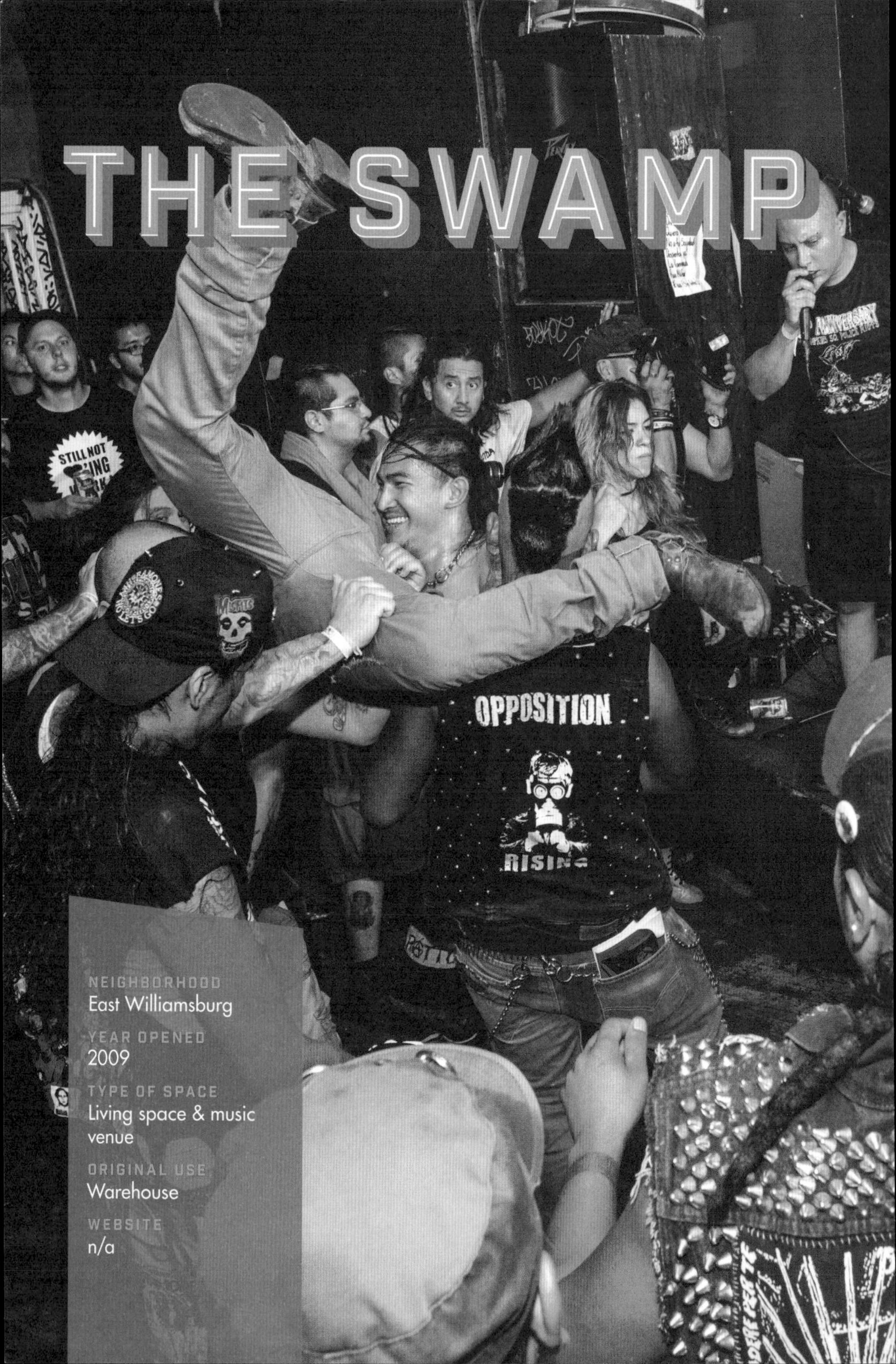

NEIGHBORHOOD
East Williamsburg

YEAR OPENED
2009

TYPE OF SPACE
Living space & music
venue

ORIGINAL USE
Warehouse

WEBSITE
n/a

**"I was lucky enough to have CBGB when I** grew up, but there's nothing like that now," says drummer Christian Erazo, who runs the Swamp. "I want to give kids a little glimpse of how punk shows used to be, and try to influence the scene in a positive way."

The Swamp is a quintessential DIY music venue: it's an unmarked industrial building on a desolate street, home to five artists and musicians, and every so often the living room fills with 100 or so gleeful punks with asymmetrical haircuts and an array of spiked accessories thrashing around to really fast, really loud music. The fare is mostly punk and hardcore—Resistant Culture, the Degenerics, Reagan Youth, Death Mold, and HR of Bad Brains—and there's also a monthly reggae night and some ska and rocksteady shows. The community drawn to the Swamp is generally radical, anarchistic, and anti-authoritarian; some shows begin with a progressive film screening, and activist groups set up tables in the kitchen to sell or give away patches, buttons, zines, mixtapes, and t-shirts.

The building was home to performance gallery Asterisk Art Space starting in 2002. Christian took over in 2009 and renamed the space the Lake, then changed it to the Swamp in 2012. "I didn't really pick the name for any particular reason," he says, "but it definitely gets swampy during shows." The Swamp is emphatically underground—no address is given anywhere online, and show flyers say NEED DIRECTIONS? ASK A PUNK. "We engage with the people who come here and let them know what the situation is," Christian says. "We want to make sure everyone understands that it's a privilege to have this place."

Booking for the space is handled by EastRev, a collective of half a dozen musicians that Christian is a part of, along with Jayson Nugget from the Slackers and Pedro Erazo from Gogol Bordello. The group has been promoting and

OPPOSITE AND ABOVE: **Scenes from the 2014 Latino Punk Fest, a three-day bonanza featuring more than 20 bands from the United States, Mexico, Columbia, and Panama, performing in four different venues.**

organizing shows around New York and New Jersey since 2006. "Our thing is not money but community," says Christian. "We have a great group of people who follow us and come to all the shows, so we try to make each one a really awesome event." Because the Swamp is a home first and a venue second, EastRev only puts on two or three shows there each month, many of which are benefits for radical groups like Anarchist Black Cross, WIN Animal Rights, NYC Antifa, and the Wolf Mountain Sanctuary.

Christian is aware of the many potential problems of running a DIY venue, and he makes it a point to get to know all his neighbors, always giving them notice about shows. He's also careful not to upset the landlord—"he's a great guy with a big heart, and he's been very open to what we do. We don't want to cause him any trouble." Christian is also very conscientious of safety and the law. "This is a place where you can do something crazy, but we want to make sure nothing bad happens as a result," he says. "Maybe someone will burn a flag during their act, which is great, but that's also why we have fire extinguishers and sprinklers."

*Photos by Walter*

CLOCKWISE FROM TOP LEFT: **Huasipungo; Christian Erazo manning the sound booth; Zines, buttons,** patches, and other merch for sale.

CLOCKWISE FROM TOP: **A sweaty, swampy audience; Konstrukt; ATRAKO.**

# TIME'S UP

**NEIGHBORHOOD**
South Williamsburg

**YEAR OPENED**
2010

**TYPE OF SPACE**
Skillshare

**ORIGINAL USE**
Bike shop

**WEBSITE**
times-up.org

**Environmental-justice nonprofit Time's Up** has been active for more than twenty-five years. Founded by Bill DiPaola on the Lower East Side in 1987, the organization was involved in many protests against the city during the 1980s and 1990s, particularly the fight to save community gardens. But bicycle advocacy is the cause for which the group is best known—they've been at the forefront of nearly every advance in the cultural visibility of cycling that the city has made in the past thirty years.

Time's Up has about 200 volunteers running dozens of campaigns and hundreds of workshops annually. "We constantly strive to keep cyclists strong," says Bill. "We focus a lot on new cyclists, helping people learn to love riding." The group began holding monthly rides in Central Park and Prospect Park in 1991, and still do about 50 themed rides a year, from clown rides to pirate rides to peace rides. Time's Up activists worked with HUB Station to found NYC's pedicab industry in 1995 and helped facilitate New York's participation in Critical Mass, a worldwide group ride that promotes cyclists' rights. In 2005 Time's Up activists started the Streets Memorial Project to raise awareness of the dangers of New York City streets to cyclists, and they helped bring the Ghost Bike Project to New York—making white-painted bicycles into street memorials to mark places cyclists have been struck and killed.

During Occupy Wall Street in 2011, Time's Up members built energy-generating bikes for protestors to use in Zucotti Park after their generators were confiscated. Though most of those bikes were destroyed by the police, the group made a dozen more immediately after Superstorm Sandy in 2012, with funding from the activist group Occupy Sandy. These were deployed as mobile charging stations on the Lower East Side and in the Rockaways, where Time's Up members also coordinated group rides to deliver donated food, clothing, and other goods.

OPPOSITE: A fraction of the recycled and reclaimed bikes that await refurbishing in the Time's Up workshop. ABOVE LEFT: Time's Up's bike part vending machine, filled with tubes, lights, and other accessories. ABOVE RIGHT: A DIY fixing session.

The group's longest-running project is their bike co-op, through which they sell upcycled and refurbished bikes as well as host classes and open-shop sessions to teach people to fix their own rides. Since 2005, one class per week has been women and trans only. "We teach cyclists skills they can use for the rest of their lives," says Bill. "They're empowering themselves, making themselves independent."

Time's Up got their first dedicated space in 2009, in the basement of long-running collective and activist center ABC No Rio. In 2010 they got a second space in South Williamsburg, in what used to be Traif Bike Gesheft—non-kosher bike shop. The space even came with a vending machine for bike accessories, now stocked with lights, pumps, and other things cyclists might need to fix themselves up in the middle of the night. Their landlord is the former owner of that shop, Baruch Herzfeld, himself a cycling advocate who seeks to bridge two of Williamsburg's very different groups: the Chasidic Jews who have lived in the area for decades and the incoming hipsters and artists. Time's Up has done significant work in that area as well: when the South Williamsburg shop opened, volunteers gave free bikes to Chasidic kids, and they were delighted to see how many Chasidic adults came to the open-shop nights. "It's really interesting to see them working alongside a bunch of hipsters who obviously have very different values," says Keegan Stephens, one of the co-op mechanics. "But everyone quickly realizes that they're not so different after all; it's just such great community building. We're all friends by the end of the night."

*Photos by Maximus and Time's Up*

During the Occupy Wall Street movement in 2011, the NYPD confiscated the generators protesters were using to power their Zucotti Park encampment. Time's Up constructed energy-generating bicycles and brought them to the park to charge cell phones, computers, and other devices.

CLOCKWISE FROM TOP: The "Running the Bulls (Out of Town)" ride, part of a protest against corrupt banks; "Love Your Lane" campaign volunteers giving hot chocolate to winter cyclists; energy bikes ready for deployment in the Rockaways after Superstorm Sandy; activists outside of ABC No Rio raising awareness of the dangers of nuclear power.

# TRANS-PECOS

NEIGHBORHOOD
Ridgewood

YEAR OPENED
2013

TYPE OF SPACE
Music venue

ORIGINAL USE
Textile factory

WEBSITE
thetranspecos.com

**Though Trans-Pecos is in Ridgewood,** Queens, it's a crucial part of Brooklyn's DIY music scene, a scene in which Todd Patrick, who runs this space, has played an integral role. Todd has had a hand in or a strong influence on an impressive number of the borough's underground music venues, and with Trans-Pecos, he is proving that DIY can grow up, become legit, integrate with the neighborhood, and remain a well-respected platform for cutting-edge music.

Todd began his New York music career in the early 2000s, booking shows in various alternative places, like parking lots, storefronts, church basements, and construction sites. Emphatically all-ages and cheap, his shows presented interesting artists and attracted a dedicated audience. At a time when Brooklyn was becoming a proving ground for musicians, Todd was booking as-yet-unknown bands that would go on to great mainstream success, including Matt and Kim, Dirty Projectors, Animal Collective, TV on the Radio, Japanther, Lightning Bolt, and the Vivian Girls.

Over the years, Todd has run several DIY music spaces, starting with the short-lived Llano Estacado on the Williamsburg waterfront in 2004. That same year he started Williamsburg underground arts and music complex Monster Island with Eric Zajaceskowski, who would go on to co-found Secret Project Robot (p. 182), running it until 2011. He also ran Bushwick DIY venue Market Hotel from 2008 until it shut down in 2010; in 2013 he got a grant to reopen it legally. He started the massively popular 285 Kent in 2010 and ushered it to a close in 2014. And he was involved in the original Silent Barn—a former textile factory in Ridgewood where a half-dozen live-in musicians threw underground shows from 2004 to 2011—which is also the origin of Trans-Pecos.

In July 2011, Silent Barn was closed down by the Department of Buildings because the tenants were illegally living in a commercially zoned building. Many of its former residents went on to form a huge, innovative collective in Bushwick (p. 186); meanwhile, Todd took over the Ridgewood space, spending two and a half years turning it into a fully licensed venue, bar, café, and community center. A few of the old Silent Barn murals remain in homage, and the original denizens' strangely shaped bedrooms now form Trans-Pecos' offices, storage rooms, and bar.

"Musically, Trans-Pecos caters to the outsider community from every stylistic, methodological, and social background, whether it's independent hip-hop, minimal techno, new music on a classical

OPPOSITE AND ABOVE: Performers and audience at the twelve-hour Escape From New York party, thrown in the summer of 2014 by the band Skeletons, who lived in this factory back in 2004.

trajectory, or noise," says Sam Hillmer, Trans-Pecos's Curatorial Director and Operations Manager and also a veteran of Brooklyn's DIY music scene; he actually played at the very first Silent Barn show under the name Regattas. Although Sam is something of a curatorial gatekeeper, Trans-Pecos is programmed by a rotating cast of about twenty bookers, rather than having one person control the space's musical personality.

In addition to innovative programming, the Trans-Pecos crew has made huge strides in neighborhood integration and community engagement. They've built relationships with local landlords and tenants, their police precinct, and their Community Affairs Officer and Special Operations Lieutenant. They've spoken with their council members and at community board meetings, and have engaged community partners like the Greater Ridgewood Youth Council and the Coalition for Hispanic Family Services. "Engagement has to manifest in practice, not just ideologically, and it has to fill a need," Sam says. The most

fully developed partnership is with the AHRC, an advocacy organization serving New York's developmentally disabled. During the day, AHRC brings artists to Trans-Pecos to write and practice music, then books many of them to perform in the evenings as well. This partnership is called the Zebulon Institute for Music and Art, named after the beloved Williamsburg bar/venue that closed in 2012.

"The best work always comes from the strongest communities of practice," Sam says. "When you have people who care about each other, and a sense of place that they share, you get strong artistic output." Trans-Pecos is making great strides to show that DIY can have a positive impact on every community it touches—the musicians, the audience, the neighborhood, and the city as a whole.

*Photos by Kit, Maximus, and Walter*

OPPOSITE, CLOCKWISE: EULA, Robot Death Kites, Push Ups. THIS PAGE, TOP: Weaves; Robot Death Kites. MIDDLE: Escape from New York party. BOTTOM: The Trans-Pecos community woodshop, where the venue's benches, tables, and stage were constructed.

# URBANGLASS

NEIGHBORHOOD
Ft. Greene

YEAR OPENED
1991

TYPE OF SPACE
Skillshare

ORIGINAL USE
Vaudeville theatre

WEBSITE
urbanglass.org

**Founded by a trio of SoHo ceramicists** in 1977 and originally called the New York Experimental Glass Workshop, UrbanGlass is now the largest studio glass facility in the country. According to Executive Director Cybele Maylone, the original mission—which still guides the nonprofit organization today—was "to give artists access to the materials, equipment, and support they need to pursue working in a medium that is out of reach for most individual artists."

With help from the NYC Economic Development Corporation, UrbanGlass crossed the East River in 1991, taking over the 17,000-square-foot third floor of the then-derelict Mark Strand Theatre, an opulent building constructed in 1918 as a vaudeville venue—according to Brooklyn real estate blog Brownstoner, "it was intended to look like an old Roman palazzo on steroids." The move was a gamble, as Ft. Greene at that time was severely underpopulated and rife with abandoned buildings, but it paid off. "We've really been part of the cultural renaissance in this neighborhood," says Cybele.

The studio facility boasts a wide range of equipment and tools for all different kinds of glasswork: "We try to speak to the material on all levels," Cybele says. There are six main areas: the kiln studio, with eleven ovens in a variety of shapes and sizes; the hot shop, with three furnaces set at 2,000°, eleven "glory holes" for heating glass and eleven annealers for cooling it; the cold shop, where cooled glass projects can be refined, polished, cut, and engraved; the mold-making studio, where artists create molds for casting projects; the flameworking and neon studio, for working on a tiny scale with a torch or bending neon tubes into various shapes; and the stained glass studio, for cutting, painting, and piecing together glass creations.

Education is a major part of UrbanGlass' focus. Says Cybele, "We want to give people the literal tools to work with glass, as well as the knowledge and skills to explore the material in all types of art-making." There's a range of classes, for beginners to professionals. All in all, 75 to 100 people pass through the facilities in a day.

UrbanGlass' equipment and coworking model are essential for aspiring glass artists, because it's virtually impossible for an individual to create a studio space to work with glass—it's legally and logistically complex, and requires a great deal of space and money.

There is also a long-running all-scholarship program called the Bead Project, which is open to low-income women who are interested in learning to make glass jewelry. The class combines studio time with classroom time, so in addition to learning how to work with glass, women are also instructed in writing business plans, approaches to marketing, and other entrepreneurial topics.

More than two decades after UrbanGlass made the Strand Theatre their home, the NYC Department of Cultural Affairs funded a $41 million top-to-bottom renovation of the space, which is now part of the thriving Downtown Brooklyn Cultural District, adjacent to BRIC Arts & Media, BAM, and many other luminaries. "Working in glass is a communal practice, and we bring artists together to support them in their work," says Cybele. "I think places like UrbanGlass definitely contribute to the very fertile landscape in Brooklyn right now."

*Photos by Alix*

CLOCKWISE: Glassblowing can be dangerous and is always done in teams; members of the Bead Project doing flamework; the 2014 Bead Project class on the last day of the program.

Artists and artisans use UrbanGlass' studio facilities in equal measure. "There are a lot of little economies here," says Executive Director Cybele Maylone.

# WATERFRONT MUSEUM

130

NEW YORK CENTRAL N° 26

NEIGHBORHOOD
Red Hook

YEAR OPENED
1985

TYPE OF SPACE
Museum

ORIGINAL USE
Cargo ship

WEBSITE
waterfrontmuseum.org

**In 1985, David Sharps bought the Lehigh** Valley Railroad Barge No. 79 for $1. The ship, built in 1914 to carry cargo into the New York Harbor, was sunk eight feet deep in the mudflats of Edgewater, NJ, and it took David two years to remove 300 tons of mud from the hull, restore the barge, and get her floating again. "I had never run a power tool in my life," David says. "My background was as a clown."

Despite his lack of ship-restoration proficiency, David has been on the water nearly his entire adult life. A self-taught juggler, by twenty-one he had an act with Carnival Cruise lines. He then went on to attend Parisian theatre school L'Ecole Jacques Lecoq, during which he was caretaker of a converted barge while its captain traveled in the Philippines. He returned to the States, and after less than a week in New York, "someone had given me a floating home." He became part of a tug and barge community in the North

Bergen Lighthouse Boat Basin, which eventually led him to the Lehigh Valley barge.

Permanently docking a huge boat isn't easy—or cheap. The North Bergen Lighthouse Boat Basin was evicted in the mid-1980s, and David started over in Edgewater with the rescue of the Lehigh Valley No. 79. Working with a group of friends and skilled carpenters, he restored the barge and turned it into a floating nonprofit museum. In addition to displays about maritime history and the story of this barge in particular, the Waterfront Museum is filled with artifacts—signboards, tools, lanterns, fittings, barrels, foghorns, bells. David has acquired very little of it on his own; "people just keep bringing me stuff," he says.

In 1989 David moved the museum to Hoboken, where it was quite popular: "The town loved us, the city council loved us; the only problem was that none of those people owned the waterfront." The arrangement in Hoboken didn't last, and

The majority of the Waterfront Museum's ephemera has been donated by fans and fellow maritime enthusiasts. OPPOSITE: A selection of lanterns that have been taken out for cleaning. ABOVE: Founder David Sharps on his barge, a floating artifact and a beautiful piece of maritime history.

the museum moved to several other temporary homes until 1994, when David met Greg O'Connell of the O'Connell Organization—a family-owned real estate company with more than 150 properties in New York, many on the Red Hook waterfront. Greg, a former NYPD officer who is known for his community-mindedness, told David: "Bring the barge over to Red Hook. We'd love to have you."

"So Brooklyn embraced us, Red Hook embraced us," says David. The Lehigh Valley No 79—a maritime museum, floating classroom, cultural programming venue, and David's home—has been docked at the end of Conover Street ever since. In twenty years it has brought hundreds of thousands of people to the waterfront, from school groups to tourists, for everything from circuses to lectures to weddings. The Red Hook community board has pointed to the Waterfront Museum as possibly the single most significant factor in bringing people to the neighborhood for the first time.

Back in 1990, *Life* magazine named Red Hook the "crack capital of America," and when David moved in, the waterfront was fairly decrepit. But with concerted effort, an ambitious group of volunteers hastened its transformation into one of the most gorgeous places in Brooklyn. "I'm so fortunate to have a port here," David says. "We have the best view of any museum in New York."

*Photos by Alix*

The museum functions as a "floating classroom," educating people of all ages about the history and future of the New York waterfront, focusing on the shipping industry and the social and engineering forces that caused barges like this one to become obsolete.

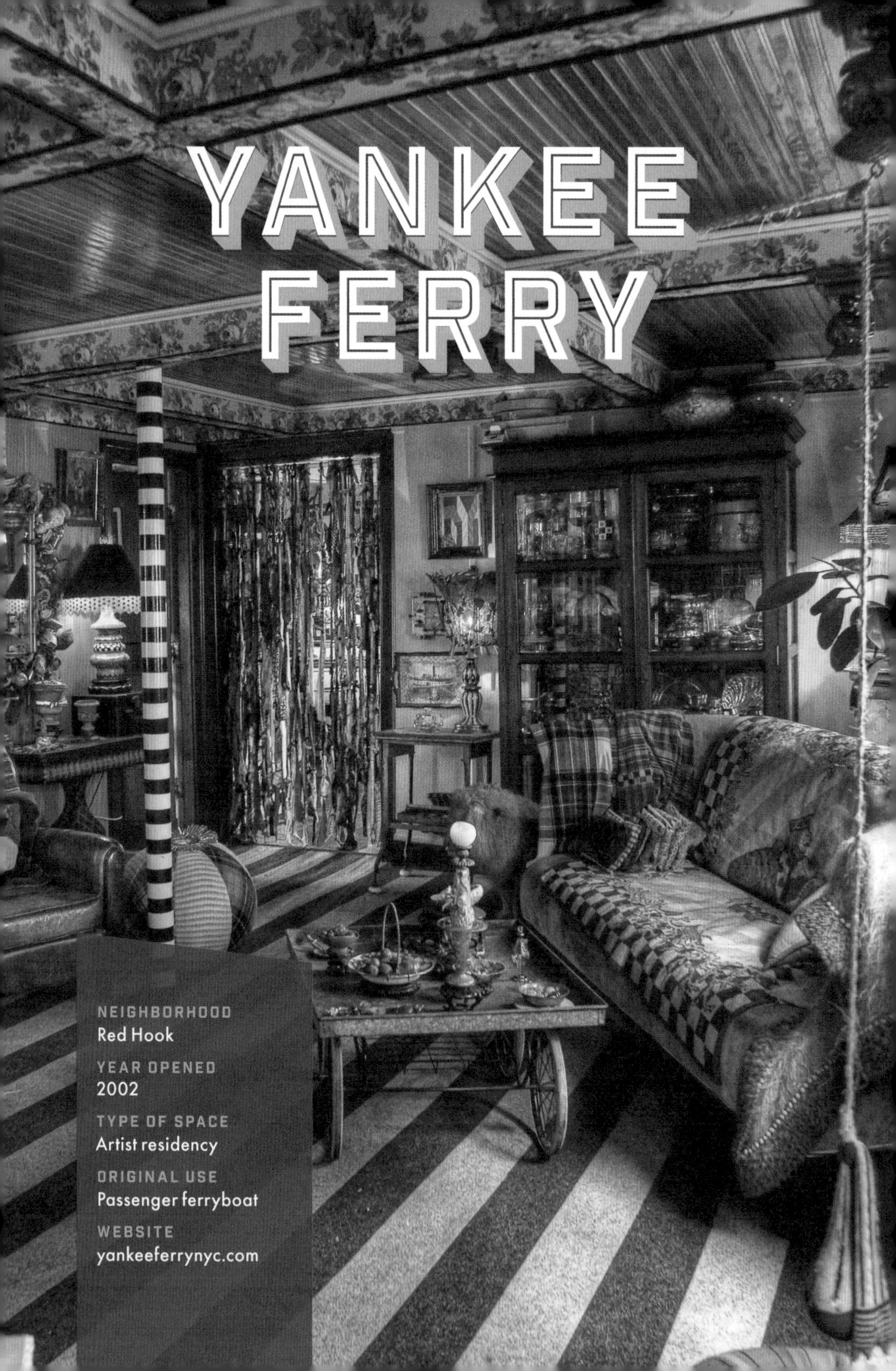

# YANKEE FERRY

NEIGHBORHOOD
Red Hook

YEAR OPENED
2002

TYPE OF SPACE
Artist residency

ORIGINAL USE
Passenger ferryboat

WEBSITE
yankeeferrynyc.com

**Yankee Ferry, one of the oldest boats on** the Eastern Seaboard, has led many lives. Built in 1907 and christened *Machigonne*, she was one of the fanciest ferryboats of her ilk, tricked out with carved mahogany, cut crystal, and mohair velvet cushions. She was put to service ferrying passengers around Maine's Calendar Islands and Massachusetts' Pines Island, but when America entered World War I, she was commissioned into the US Navy, painted battleship grey, armed with cannons, and sent to war. After a rugged stint of duty, she spent a decade carrying immigrants into Ellis Island and bringing tourists to the Statue of Liberty, until World War II began and she was once again armed to serve. After that war, her engine was upgraded and she was rechristened *Yankee*. For the next forty years she was used as a "daddy boat," bringing men back and forth between Providence, RI, where they worked, and Block Island, where they lived with their families.

"Ships are built for a particular waterway and service, but Yankee just kept changing," says Victoria MacKenzie-Childs, who stewards her now. "She became a kind of a hodgepodge or mosaic—things were added on, taken off, stripped down." In rough shape by 1990, Yankee was restored by Jim Gallagher, an antiques dealer from Louisiana, who also facilitated her acceptance into the National Register of Historic Places. He docked her in Tribeca for nearly a decade, and she became a beloved fixture in the neighborhood.

Enter Victoria and her husband Richard: artists, sculptors, and creators and former owners of the MacKenzie-Childs line of fanciful, rustic home furnishings. Victoria had been thinking for some time about a houseboat, and was thrilled when she heard there was a ferry for sale. "So I strapped on my skates and went down to pier twenty-five," she says. By early 2002, Victoria and Richard had acquired Yankee, and they

*Yankee* was constructed by the Philadelphia shipbuilding and engineering firm Neafie & Levy. She was originally called *Machigonne*, which means "on bended knee." Boats like this were built to last only a few decades, but *Yankee* has been going strong for more than a century.

took to it with characteristic exuberance, re-upholstering, repainting, refurbishing, amassing rusty bits and brightly colored bobs, making the vessel into a floating folk-art fairytale. Nearly everything onboard has been found, upcycled, or inherited. "People say, 'Doesn't it cost a lot of money to take care of a boat?' And I say, 'Not if you don't have it,'" Victoria says.

But New York City is not an easy place to dock a 9,000-square-foot ferry. In 2003 the Tribeca pier was demolished, and *Yankee* was sent away. After towing her to New Jersey (the boat's engine is no longer functional), invited by the Hoboken Historical Museum, Victoria and Richard continued with their floating art project. From time to time they lowered the gangplank and rented beds to international visitors in a stay-aboard program that received top ratings across the board, from CNN to travel.com. But after eight years Hoboken's powers that be decided they no longer had room for *Yankee*, and Victoria and Richard scrambled to move again. This time they found someone willing to give them a permanent home: concrete magnate

John Quadrozzi, Jr., who owns the Gowanus Bay Terminal in South Red Hook. "He has been absolutely wonderful," Victoria says. "He really appreciates *Yankee* and all she stands for."

Now Victoria and Richard plan to turn the vessel into a floating think tank. "When people walk aboard, it changes them," Victoria says. Yankee has been visited by international CEOs, UN political affairs officers, and an entire Columbia University urban planning master's class, and everyone reports that being onboard has helped expand their thinking. "Yankee used to serve the world by moving people around," Victoria says. "Now she's ready to help by moving thought forward."

*Photos by Julia*

In addition to Victoria (above), Richard, and a rotating cast of shipmates and deckhands, *Yankee* also houses two cats, a dog, and six chickens living in coop hand-built into the prow of the boat.

Victoria and Richard MacKenzie-Childs have filled *Yankee* with myriad creative and functional flourishes, such as a bed canopy made from a huge painting and a crocheted shawl, a silverware caddy that descends via pulley to save space, and a dining table suspended from the ceiling so that it won't sway with the boat's motion.

# ACKNOWLEDGMENTS

Although I'd been doing brooklyn-spaces.com for several years, I was hardly prepared for the intensity of creating a book. This has been a very interactive project, and I am immensely grateful to all the passionate, creative people who run these spaces for sharing their lives with me, for relating their dreams, aspirations, and struggles, and for allowing me to document their stories.

I am also incredibly honored to have been able to work closely with so many astonishingly skilled photographers, who dedicated their time and talent to this project with an intensity and kindness that inspired me every step of the way. The bulk of this book was put together in a very short time, during which I sent them to all corners of the borough, often with absurdly little notice. Everyone produced absolutely stunning work, giving each space all the attention and care it deserved.

Maximus Comissar (maximuscommissar.com) and Alix Piorun (alixpiorun.com) have partnered with me on brooklyn-spaces.com for several years. Cameras at the ready, they've followed me to a nearly endless parade of performance extravaganzas, underground dance parties, visual art exhibitions, and music shows, smiling (mostly) all the while. This book definitely would not exist without their incredible work, and my life would be significantly duller without them. Walter Wlodarczyk (walterwlodarczyk.com) and Kit Crenshaw (kitcrenshaw.com) joined the project partway through and immediately made themselves indispensible. The variety and vibrancy of their work is thrilling, and I am so grateful for their willingness to completely disrupt their lives and rush out to photograph a midnight rock show or chickpea-wrestling match or DNA barcoding workshop.

Shannon Carroll (shannonleecarroll.com), Remi Pann, Ventiko (ventiko.com), Julia Roberts (jrstudios.cc), and Patricia Malfitano (patriciamalfitano.com) each generously accompanied me to one or several spaces, photographing these diverse creative hubs with enthusiasm and flair. This book also includes terrific images from Michael Blase (lowereastphoto.com), Erica Camille (ericacamilleproductions.com), Michael Connor, Simon Courchel (simoncourchel.com), Jeff Evans, Linus Gelber, Jon Handel (gustoNY. com), Nicki Ishmael (nickiishmael.com), Andrew Janke, Ruvi Leider (ruvi-leider.squarespace.com), Jen Messier, Tanya Pann, Tod Seelie (todseelie.com), and Hanne Tierney. I am so lucky to be able to feature their fantastic work.

I am extremely grateful to my agent Ellen Scordato and everyone at Stonesong for championing this project, working with me to make it stronger, and helping me find a home for it at Monacelli. I'm terrifically thankful to Stacee Lawrence and Alan Rapp at Monacelli: Stacee for seeing the project's potential and Alan for coaching me, playing cheerleader and taskmaster both, and knowing when I needed each. Thanks also to Suzanne LaGasa for her beautiful design work and for putting up with my endless frantic changes.

Finally, thank you to all my wonderful activity partners for letting me drag them out to a million spaces and events for "research," and especially to my sister Laurel, my staunchest ally and most essential coconspirator, for pushing me to start this project and for endlessly believing in everything I do—and also for teaching me that everything is better if you bike there.